PATHOS
OF
POWER

PATHOS
OF
POWER

Kenneth B. Clark

HARPER & ROW, PUBLISHERS

NEW YORK   EVANSTON   SAN FRANCISCO   LONDON

Library of Congress Cataloging in Publication Data

Clark, Kenneth Bancroft
    Pathos of power. *see slip*
    1. Power (Social sciences)   2. United States—
Social conditions.   3. Social ethics.   4. Social
scientists.   I. Title.
HN65.C53   155.2'34   73–14250
ISBN 0–06–010799–5

To Muds
Who lives a concern

CONTENTS

FOREWORD

IN AUGUST 1945, military personnel of the United States dropped an atomic bomb on the civilian population of Hiroshima. My immediate reaction was complicated bewilderment. I was starkly aware that hundreds of thousands of human beings had been destroyed by this single volitional act of warfare; my awareness was compounded and confused by a sense that this mass destruction of human beings was qualitatively different from all earlier forms of military destruction. In my turbulent attempts to understand what the United States had inflicted upon the Japanese people and the rest of humanity there remained a permeating sense of personal and collective guilt. But the justification for this personal guilt was defiantly illusive. I was tempted, almost successfully, to accept the common rationalizations against collective guilt—"this saved American lives"; "this shortened the War"; "this is no different from other forms of bombing of civilian populations in World War I and World War II."

These rationalizations would not work for me. The moral and ethical questions became more intense and more clear. They became for me the fundamental reality of the atomic and nuclear age. The dark yet blinding mushroom cloud of atomic destruction at Hiroshima and Nagasaki is a symbol of the new capacity of man to unleash total destruction upon his fellow human beings. This visible emblem demands re-examination of all past ideological, moral, and ethical premises. Its mocking reality requires a redefinition of the "realistic," the "practical," even the "imperative" in human affairs.

I found myself re-examining my ideas about the characteristics of human beings; the problems of justice and injustices; possible safeguards against human cruelties; the role of religion, philosophy, and science as realistic, moral, and practical barriers to human chaos and ultimate destructiveness. I had previously thought about these questions somewhat leisurely and abstractly; now they increasingly dominated my thinking with a persistence and intensity that frequently interfered with clarity and coherence.

This book is adapted from papers I have written over the past quarter of a century in an attempt to clarify my thoughts about the awesome confrontation of a nuclear age. The fact is that I have been writing this book about the complexities of human personal and social interaction throughout my professional and personal life. This book presents to its readers all of the risks involved in exposing a distillation of one's thinking about problems that are by their essential nature difficult to define and focus. It reveals the continuities and betrays the inconsistencies and the rigidities of my ideas about the responsibility of concerned and thoughtful individuals to try to make the quality of human life more endurable. It represents the particular perspectives and biases of a social psychologist who has insisted on stating his bias that the social sciences are the sciences of human morality and, therefore, must state and deal with values; and who has declared his faith that disciplined human intelligence and the use of man's capacity for rational thought are the foundations for functional social sciences and for that practical morality which is essential for human survival.

As I reread this book I was disturbed by the fact that the bringing together of articles that were written over a period of time, for different audiences, seemed almost to bludgeon my readers, my fellow human beings. The glaring flaws of a seeming lack of compassion, an absence of empathy—a lack of that positive identification which is essential for the broader perspective of man—seemed less stark in separate articles than they seemed to me when my reflections were joined in this book. There were many times when I seriously questioned the advisability of publishing at all. I made the decision to publish because this book does reflect what I have thought and believe. It is an accurate, though partial, expression of my thoughts over time; the papers exist; they are a reality. Above all I could not avoid the very clear risk of misunderstanding and ridicule by withdrawal without at the same time accepting the fact that I had succumbed to personal cowardice.

A social diagnostician inevitably runs the risk of a preoccupation with the negatives in human affairs; but if the negatives are the only realities and the inevitable determinants of the future, then there is no purpose in seeking to communicate with one's fellow human beings about problems of social justice and social morality and social responsibility. If negatives alone will determine the future of man, writing books on the nature of man and the complexities of human society is a futile gesture. That social philosophers write speeches and articles and books at all is evidence of the persistence of the necessary functional optimism, the belief that human beings do have positive potentials which it is possible to tap, to stimulate, and to make dominant.

When my students have accused me of a debilitating and immobilizing pessimism, I have responded by pointing out to them that they could not possibly be right, or else I would not be engaging in the dialogues and discourses of the classroom. This book also is an expression of hope and of faith in the possibility that human beings can achieve a practical morality essential to the survival of the human species.

I base my faith and my hope in that functional morality on the capacity of the behavioral sciences to provide the necessary knowledge and technology to counteract the threats abruptly imposed upon us by the amoral intellectual contributions of the physical sciences. I place the burden of demonstrating the validity of this hope on the shoulders of social science colleagues who have been arrogant enough and optimistic enough to presume to work in that complicated, frustrating field that tries to understand the dynamics and turbulences of the human personality and human society. I ask of them that they share with me the belief that their choice in this use of their intelligence and their training brings with it an obligation to develop the behavioral sciences with that clarity, precision, and sensitivity required for an effective moral technology.

In making this request I am fully aware that the behavioral sciences do not now, in a nuclear age, have the leisure available in the past to the physical and biological sciences. One of the disturbing legacies of the nuclear age is that time has been threateningly accelerated. This barrier of limited and accelerated time must be overcome. The formidable power alignments, the vested interests, and group identifications must somehow be neutralized. They must be overcome by a human intelligence propelled by a sense of the urgency of survival in a time when the stakes are ultimate.

In making this plea for social responsibility among behavioral scientists and in asserting that moral and ethical concerns are no longer physical abstractions but have now become absolutely necessary for the ultimate practicality—the survival of the human species—one necessarily presents oneself as social critic. This is an awkward, embarrassing, and seemingly arrogant role. The social critic can, with some justification, be accused of divorcing himself from the frailties of his fellow man. Too often, social criticism is afflicted with a humorless dogmatism and egocentric fanaticism, which can justify rejection and cruelty to "less worthy" others. These moral and ego pitfalls must be avoided by behavioral scientists who accept the burden and the obligation of seeking to help the human species to survive. The social critic must avoid becoming indistinguishable from those whom he criticizes. In the search for safeguards against these dangers, I have struggled to understand how social criticism can be constructive. Criticism cannot become one more excuse for destructive polarizations among men. I have come, at this stage of my life, to the conclusion that the antidotes are embarrassingly simple—humor, empathy, compassion, and kindness.

Humor is an important gyroscope too often neglected in serious discussions of human affairs. I have read that one of the first qualities which the seriously neurotic and psychotic patient loses is the sense of humor. It has occurred to me that I have never met a dogmatist or a person who made me afraid who had a sense of humor. Even "sick" humor is curiously reassuring. Humor is not necessarily, overtly, laughter. It is more complex than joy. Humor is leavening that reflects a perspective beyond narrow egocentric preoccupations. It is an acceptance of the inconsistencies, the transitoriness, the frailties, the pretensions, the genuine feelings, the inescapable absurdities—and, above all, the mocking embarrassment—that is inherent in being a conscious human being. Humor puts the ego in perspective; it demands that if man accepts himself—respects himself and his fellow man —he must do so with a totality of acceptance. Humor unmasks pretense. Humor reminds us that we are mortal, that we are mere, awesome, awkward human beings. A social critic without humor can be saved from the self-contradiction of dogmatism only through the help, compassion, and kindness of others who share his values and goals.

Empathy, like humor, has the capacity to identify with the joy, the anguish, the aspirations, the defeats, and the transitory successes of other human beings. Empathy brings psychological cohesion. It demonstrates the interdependence, the oneness of mankind. And compassion is the functional manifestation of empathy.

In one of his most beautiful essays, Bertrand Russell said that if he were to be asked what he considered to be the most important single answer to the solution of human problems—personal, social, and international—he would be embarrassed to give the answer because it is so simple. It is kindness. Kindness is not a lazy tolerance. Kindness requires courage; the courage to express and accept love; the courage to resist the blandness, passivity, or condescensions which betray a basic indifference to the positive capacity of others; and kindness demands the courage to believe in and accept the totality of another and to help a human being dare to be that which is good within him. This is the kindness that I believe could save the world from mindless, tragic nothingness.

Kenneth B. Clark

Hastings-on-Hudson
February 1974

ACKNOWLEDGMENTS

For the prologue, I have adapted some of my remarks at the 43rd Annual Congress of Cities in Las Vegas, 1966, when I spoke on the topic "Cities for Man—Man's Hope for Richness of Real Community"; excerpts from an address "Respect for Man—The Unqualifiable Basis for Unity" at the Conference on National Unity, Sterling Forest Gardens, New York, November, 1969; and excerpts from a paper entitled "Everyday Life and Social Identity" at the Smithsonian Institution International Symposium, November, 1970, to be included in the forthcoming book *The Cultural Drama: Interpretations of Diversity, Identity and Protest*, edited by Wilton S. Dillon (Washington, D.C., 1974). I developed a number of these same ideas in the fall of 1967 at Marymount College and at Colby Junior College, and in October, 1968, in my address "The Future of Our Cities" at The Mills College Convocation at Oakland.

Chapter 1 is a paper entitled "The Negro Intellectual in Contemporary America," delivered in July 1961, on acceptance of the 46th Spingarn Medal at the 52nd Annual Convention of the National Association for the Advancement of Colored People in Philadelphia.

Chapter 2 draws on several sources but primarily on an address "Some Problems of Human Intelligence" before the Gamma Chapter of Phi Beta Kappa, November 1964, in New York, reprinted in *American Scholar* as "Intelligence, the University and Society" (Vol. 36, Winter 1966–67). I have also quoted from unpublished papers, including "Dilemma of Intelligence in the Contemporary World," written in the late 1940s, and "The Paradox of Human Intelligence," written in 1964; from my Hunter College Centennial address, February 1970, reprinted as "The Governance of Universities in the Cities of Man" in *American Scholar* (Vol. 39, Autumn 1970); and a commencement address entitled "Toward a Defense of 'Non-Relevant' Education," delivered at Amherst College, June 1969.

Chapter 3 is adapted from a paper "Social Science and Social Tensions," presented to the 38th Annual Meeting of the National Committee for Mental Hygiene, New York, November 1947, reprinted in *Mental Hygiene* (Vol. 32, January 1948).

Chapter 4 is the Kurt Lewin Memorial Award Address entitled "Problems of Power and Social Change: Toward a Relevant Social Psychology," given before the Society for the Psychological Study of Social Issues, at the American Psychological Association, Chicago, September 1965, reprinted in *The Journal of Social Issues* (Vol. 21, July 1965). It also draws from a speech in May 1967 before Pennsylvania State University on "The Necessity of Inter-Disciplinary Coordination in Policy-Making and Action-Oriented Programs."

Chapter 5 includes some of the later sections of my introduction, "The Social Scientists, The Brown Decision and Contemporary Confusion," prepared for *Argument: The Oral Argument Before the Supreme Court in Brown vs. Board of Education of Topeka 1952–55*, edited by Leon Friedman (New York, 1969); and unpublished reflections called "Social Psychology and the Law in the Public School Desegregation Cases," probably written in 1955 for a Chicago meeting of The National Urban League.

Chapter 6 draws primarily from a speech "The Social Scientists: Social Critics or Social Apologists?" before the New York Chapter of Phi Beta Kappa, New York, June 1973. It also includes excerpts from a radio address (Bavarian Broadcasting System) "How Sick Is America?" Munich, July 1973, reprinted in the book, *Wie Krank Ist Amerika?* edited by Willy Hochkeppel (Hamburg, 1973); a speech entitled "American Morality and Our Cities," delivered at Cooper Union Forum, New York, November 1972; and "Social Policy, Power and Social Science Research," an article published in *The Harvard Educational Review* (Vol. 43, February 1973). Similar ideas were discussed in a speech called "Social Power and Social Change in Contemporary America," before summer interns of the U.S. Department of State, Agency for International Development and the U.S. Information Agency in Washington, D.C., July 1966.

Chapter 7 is based on my address at the November 1970 Smithsonian Institution International Symposium, previously mentioned; on "Psychology and Social Responsibility: Toward a Scientific Ethic," a paper presented to the American Psychological Association's board of directors, December 1970; on "The Rehumanization of Psychology: A Contemporary Imperative," an address given before the Massachusetts Psychological Association at Boston College, May 1971, reprinted in *The Massachusetts Psychological Association Newsletter* (Vol. 15, June 1971); and on an address before the Alumni Association of the New York University School of Education, October 1970.

The Epilogue is an expanded version of the Presidential Address, which was delivered before the American Psychological Association, Washington, D.C., September 4, 1971, and reprinted in *The American Psychologist* (Vol. 26, December 1971).

Although some of these writings have been condensed or excerpted from their original sources for this book, the editing of passages used has been confined to style and has not altered substance. Within each of the parts of this book, my exploration of a theme is presented essentially in chronological order as I developed it.

Special personal thanks must be expressed to Jennifer Gerard, my editor's assistant; Cathy Clark, my secretary; and Susan Phillis, the librarian at MARC. These three kind, competent, and concerned human beings assumed and carried through the arduous tasks of checking sources, arranging copyrights, and transforming mangled copy into a typed coherence which seemed miraculous. Their individual and concerted concern with details made it possible to produce a book from articles that were widely separated in time and space.

For the past twenty years, Jeannette Hopkins has been my editor, my goad, and my friend. The existence of this book more than any other that I have written reveals the complexity and the many dimensions of her role in having the courage to continue to work with me in spite of my own incorrigible qualities. Because she never doubted, because she insisted in the face of my doubts, *Pathos of Power* became a book.

K.B.C.

PROLOGUE

THE JOKE

CONSCIOUSNESS IS an artifact—the most important artifact of the universe—a consequence of the unique evolutionary complexity of the structure and function and biochemical interaction of the billions of cortical cells which constitute the human brain. It is threatening and intolerable to know this. Ironically, the cortical cells themselves insist on denial; the human being clings to a compensatory arrogance, asserting that he is God-like, God-creating, God-obeying, God-defying; he creates social, philosophical, and political systems to proclaim his primacy over all other systems of matter and energy—living and inanimate—in the universe. He builds elaborate systems of rationalizations to "prove" his superiority over other men. He insists upon his immortality despite overwhelming empirical evidence to the contrary.

Man's creations are the most persuasive support for the worth and substance of his ego. Man transforms his ideas and hopes into things. He controls and manipulates his environment to meet his biological and ideational needs and

[3]

to control his fears. He makes tools and weapons, builds shelters and temples, neighborhoods and cities. He organizes armies and hierarchies to preserve what he has built. His civilization seeks to give substance and immortality to his fragile and mortal ego. This is the grandeur—and the pathos —of man.

Man is that thinking, feeling, searching animal who in his most developed state demands gratification not only of biological needs but also of the needs of the mind and spirit. His restless search to validate his existence is not satisfied by acquisition. It is one of the wondrous ironies of man—the human joke—that the futilities of the biological approach to human affirmation are seldom recognized or understood until the need is assuaged. Though the biological, the sensual, the material are necessary for life, their illusiveness emerges with mocking clarity only when they are attained.

The legend of Midas points to this profound and terrifying human predicament. Only a successful man who has mastered the more concrete demands and challenges of his environment can know the depths of human despair and frustration. Only the affluent, the materially and militarily powerful nation knows the loneliness of pomp and the pretense of power. The Midas syndrome is the bequest of the practical joker who designed the human predicament: the successful man and the successful nation alone can experience the fullest despair.

Where the promises of material and ideological, democratic and socialist utopias have almost been fulfilled for the majority, "identity crisis," "alienation," "existential ennui" become fashionable phrases of sophisticated contemporary discourse. "Urban unrest," "riots," "rebellions," "anticolonial movements," "black liberation," "women's liberation," "gay liberation," "student liberation" reflect the anger of realization that the promises of personal and social identity have not been kept. The end of colonialism, expanded education for the masses, the production of more telephones, more washing machines, more airplanes, better wages and more leisure, larger libraries with more books and more lavishly equipped museums, all encouraged expectations that remain unfulfilled.

The deprived and rejected maintain the illusion that to get what they lack will give life substance. The meaning of life is in the process of struggling. Each acquisition, each success, becomes a triumph that compensates for each failure. The balance is the concrete index of the worth of a lifetime.

For the undeveloped or developing nations, or regions of our own nation, the goals are equally simple and the measures of success and failure equally direct and concrete: an increase in food, a raising of the material standard of living, and industrial, technological, and military growth will determine the effectiveness of the political system and the tenure of office of political managers. Until immediate and concrete needs are met, man does not dare to recognize even more urgent and uniquely human demands—the desires and the insistencies of the human brain and the human heart which he describes as "the spirit," "the soul," "God."

It neither adds to nor subtracts from the urgency of these unavoidable spiritual needs to debate whether man creates his own needs. Man differentiates himself from other forms of life, and this ability gives his "spirit" validity. He creates and worships, writes and paints; he sculpts and dances and sings; he argues and fights. And this gives his needs affirmation. He will fast or reject a willing mate to preserve his spiritual needs, and when necessary he will kill and be killed for them.

No plan for man which views man merely as a food-, shelter-, and mate-seeking *animal* can be responsive to the totality of man the human being. Man insists upon being more than a competent animal. After the external requirements of justice and humanity are won, a creative sense of self has still to be gained.

Man is divided within himself; he is both a predatory animal and a sensitive, moral, aspiring ethical human being. Man the animal is primitive, barbaric, egocentric. The Freudian id and the Hobbesian man cannot be ignored. But, burdened with a reflective and introspective consciousness, contemporary man knows that the Darwinian interpretation of life is no longer adequate. If the human species could have depended on the imperative of the jungle it would not have been necessary to risk the anguish of the moral and sensitive response.

The evolution of the human brain made possible and demanded thought and introspection, the emergence of an awareness of responsibility for others, the development of the superego. Man observed the prolonged dependence of the infant and the dependence of the handicapped, the ill, the aged, and the infirm upon the benevolence and the empathy of the strong. Once man began to think and to feel, he could no longer reject those who were weak. Sensitivity, responsiveness, and moral confusion were the result; so were embarrassment, doubt, and a pervasive sense of inferiority and insecurity. The human predicament includes all of these. The needs for identification and unity within the tribe and empathy among all men conflict with the simple biological imperatives—the demand for human unity and universal identification competes with the demand for personal survival and disunity. The tension between them saps the energies of individuals and provokes disequilibrium among and within groups of men. Disunity, violence, injustice, cruelty—the total pattern of man's inhumanity to man—must now be understood if adaptive unity is to be achieved. Anguish, conflicts and inconsistencies, irrationalities and frailties, and aspirations reflect the human predicament.

Human groups which seek resolution through the dominance of the primitive and the animalistic cannot survive. Cannibalistic societies, societies dominated by ruthless cruelties and sacrifices, unregulated hostilities and aggressions were, and are, doomed. The increasingly complex human brain determined the search for social morality; functional ethics has an organismic base, it is a biological imperative for man.

Man's preoccupation with defining "truth" and "justice" is an attempt to concretize what is "good" and an essential step in his tortuous struggle to increase the chances of the survival of the species. The Judeo-Christian approach imposed the additional and disturbing burden of man's responsibility for man on an already morally conflicted human society. It subordinated the tyrannical role of mysticism and escape, magic, and sadism which had dominated religious thought and ritual; the sense of responsibility for other human beings became the price to be paid for the protection of God. It became the basis for human unity and the stimulus for political, social, and economic ethics.

Our future societies will either manifest the triumphant struggle and quest of the human spirit for freedom and fulfillment, or they will imprison, constrict, and dehumanize man on prefabricated altars of monotony and insensitivity. It is a central human paradox that man's ability to create an environment responsive to human needs is determined by the extent to which he is permitted to sense, to respect, and to respond to his own humanity and the humanity of others without embarrassment, apology, and awkwardness.

Real progress comes—a community enriched and a civilization of depth and substance—when some human beings insist that the created environment reflect a respect for that which is human in man. Initially, such persons speak vaguely and abstractly. They talk of values, aesthetics, and ethics, thus irritating the practical men of affairs, who above all are direct, coherent, concrete, and, if need be, ruthless.

The men of action want to get things done. There are x number of housing units that must be built; x number of schools to be planned and designed with x number of classroom units to educate the growing number of school-age children in a given community; industrial parks and shopping centers to be built and maintained; and roads and transportation to be provided to link these necessary parts of a viable economic and social community.

Those who argue that plans must be responsive to the vision and the profound reality of humanity are at a disadvantage. They cannot produce charts, profits, dividends, or other immediately quantifiable indices of value. Production, distribution, and consumption of goods and services do not seem directly related to the humanist's concern with the relationship between the environment of man and the opportunities for the pursuit and occasional fulfillment of his dreams. They cannot cite the computer.

But, the dreamer must persist in communicating his ideas to the men of power who determine the destiny of others.

Whether or not the practical men can be persuaded to listen to the conviction that only dreams are practical and that plans without dreams are doomed, the dreamers will continue to dream. They have no choice. They must respond to the inadequacy of what is by imagining and struggling for what could be.

In this spirit one dares to dream of communities that are monuments to the capacity of man to revere life and to respect his fellow human being as the only basis for self-respect; communities that cherish and nurture human intelligence, art, the sense of beauty, music, and poetry; communities that free the human imagination and permit the human spirit to commune with the God of infinite mystery and of good.

Housing in a genuine community cannot be a cage within which human beings are confined for the convenience of builders and tax assessors. Such constriction of the human spirit, only minimally reflected in the unwillingness of these prisoners to permit those who differ in color, religion, ethnic background, age, or income to share other cells of their compounds, is ironic evidence of the modifiability of the human organism. It makes an artificial virtue out of the symbols and the realities of despair.

It is difficult to conceive of the concept of man that guided one architect to design a windowless school for the center of New York City's ghetto, a building that is a concrete symbol of the prison—the no-exit—of the ghetto experience. Each day the child enters a building that tells him that he is walled in—that it is his destiny to be sentenced to the perpetual confinement of the prisons of America's dark ghettos. This architectural blunder is made all the more shocking by official explanations that, beyond eliminating the cost of replacement of windows broken by vandals, a windowless school would block the child's view of the filth and neglect of ghetto life. Yet it is the right of a child to look out of a classroom window, permitting his imagination to dream of the wonder that lies beyond the walls of that room and beyond the words and limitations of the teacher. Education is a means of looking out beyond the boundaries of the immediate. To constrain the eye of the child is to constrain the imagination and the mind.

Splendor, affluence, vulgar and tasteless displays of wealth cannot coexist with filth, neglect, squalor, and criminal and remediable human degradation in real communities. Such mockery denies humanity to all human beings. Some human beings cannot be condemned to lives of despairing ineffectualness and degradation while others are endowed with status and significant work. The real power and meaning of privilege must be measured by the quality of the life of the most lowly.

Human intelligence in the service of technology and human social engineering has made possible as the first step in human reformation the satisfaction of the minimal material needs of man for adequate food, housing, cleanliness, protection from disease and crime, resources for that security and dignity essential for human life and growth. Only understanding and commitment are necessary to obtain them.

But genuine communities must plan also for the less tangible needs of man. The richness of a real community must provide education that accepts as its primary goal the training and strengthening of man's empathic capacity—man's ability to be identified functionally with the human needs of his fellow man. It must free man to test the range of his imagination and intellect. It must prepare man for creative and meaningful work that will contribute to the needs of others; it must prepare man for constructive leisure as the basis for creative human relationships.

Our business and industrial executives and our economists must know that few men now can affirm themselves through work—although much of man's identity is still determined by work. They must plan for work as a compatible and integral part of leisure and home and education so that man of the future can live an integrated life of substance and meaning. Human intelligence, industrialization, and technology have now freed most men from the necessity of determining identity and worth through their labors, but man's hope for the richness of a real community cannot be fulfilled if he is to be burdened by guilt and shame because his life is defined by labor or the product of his training and skill. Psychology must now prepare the man of mandatory leisure to accept himself as worthy and to live creatively and joyfully and in harmony with his fellow man. The standards of worth must now be based upon values of the human being other than the criteria of the past. Within such a dynamic and creative environment, man can learn how to give and accept that love of his fellow human beings that derives strength from compassion for human frailties and limitations as much as it does from human grandeur. The anguish and ache in the human soul can be transformed through that beauty of community of purpose and dignity.

Man has the intellect and the capacity to develop cities of the future that are responsive to and stimulate the soaring human spirit and the empathic quests for human communication, interaction, and love. The cities of the future can be so beautiful that they bring out the beauty in man. Man can transform his chaotic or lawless or indifferent environment into the truly rich communities that reflect man's respect for himself, his fellow man, and his God. Those who have not already been irrevocably constricted by greed or damaged by the squalor of neglect or blind privilege or desensitized by the monotony and chronic inefficient efficiency of our cities are obligated to dream and to build such a society. Only communities of beauty and poetry and justice and love will be worthy of the beauty and poetry and love which are the potential within each human child. The boldest dreams are our only hope for a real community—our basis for survival.

But the bold dreams which alone can save us are not the reality of our lives. Our success is technological. If such success could give substance to the human ego, man's doubts and tensions, his cruelty and violence would have been resolved. Man would have achieved calm and inner security and a stable sense of identity. His society would indeed be one of peace and justice and beauty. His everyday life would be a reflection of creative and dynamic contentment.

As long as respect for human rights is not a clear and concrete reality, it is paradoxically the basis of disunity. Human beings seek to control those primitive forces responsible for man's inhumanity to man but are caught in a continuing struggle against the immoral use of power. The right of any group of human beings to impose their will upon other human beings must be restrained, and it must be restrained by means consistent with morality, without resorting to methods that violate human respect, human dignity, and human life. In attaining the means we have found the ends even more remote. This is a mocking psychological joke. Human beings who believe in ideologies and utopias, who have learned to work to make dreams real, are not prepared to endure it.

The joke is impossible to escape. We know that Harlem and Biafra and Vietnam are intolerable because television and radios and newspapers and magazines force us to know it. We become accessories to the cold murder of one human being by another when television presents the experience in the privacy of our homes. The instruments of civilization reveal the absence of civilization. Cruelty is now more disturbing because we have been taught to believe that it is remediable.

Man can communicate across space instantaneously, but he cannot communicate across the distances of national interest, race, religion, sex, or age.

This is the anguished, identity-destroying burden which youth throughout the world seek to avoid through rebellions, communes, rock festivals, by return to primitive religions, by "now cultures," by defiance and rejection of the values and standards of the past, by ridicule of adult ideologies and mocking of adult hypocrisies, and by escape through drugs, passivity, and inner emptiness. The first generation that has been required to grow under the shadow of imminent extinction has rejected the laws of rationality and the value of values while judging their elders' corruption of reason and justice. It condemns the misuse of values, yet seems to have no values.

Indeed, those who rebel against injustices are themselves often unjust. Those who scorn the consequences of dogmatism are frequently themselves blindly dogmatic. Those who are disturbed by cruelty believe that this justifies their own cruelty. Those who are frustrated by inhumane irrationality are often mindlessly irrational. Human beings concerned about the insensitivity and violence of others resort to insensitive violence to bring about a more moral system. Individuals seek identity through simplistic premises, by accepting dogmatism. Theirs is the uncritical assumption that individual human beings are expendable in the interest of some higher cause, that a higher morality justifies transitional immorality. As a President said in excusing the corruption of his administration, they operate with zeal for a cause in which they deeply believe.

Some avoid even the appearance of moral commitment by refusing to be committed, accepting the injustices of contemporary life as given, concentrating on isolated peace and personal success, accepting personal achievements and acquisitions as the measure of identity, accepting a collective identity as the measure of individual worth. The mass-produced buildings of affluence, the mass-produced slums, the mass-produced suburbia, the mass-produced drug pathology, the mass pathology of collective death in warfare all intensify tribalism, parochialism, nationalism, and racism and deny an affirmative sense of self-respect for the humanity of other human beings.

It is a truism, embarrassing to assert, that only human beings who lack respect for self and others could permit slums and ghettos to exist when they are correctable; could permit human beings to live in houses and neighborhoods of filth and ugliness when this is correctable; could permit generation after generation of human beings to be destroyed by an indifferent and inefficient educational system; could permit a soulless higher education and inner-city illiteracy; could permit pervasive cynical corruption in the heart of government; could permit art, literature, and media to become bound to commercial determinants, symbols of the hollowness and mockery of the human soul; could permit disease, death of the body and the soul in the midst of the knowledge that could heal; could assert the holiness of environmental conservation while human beings are wasted.

These are not paradoxes. The negatives of the one determine the negatives of the other; unreversed, they will increase geometrically.

A transformation of means is essential if the perception of everyday life is to be changed from negation and guilt to affirmation and esteem. We must build in human beings a sense of their own finiteness, their own limitation. Paradoxically, this is an integral part of affirmation. The fulfillment of man's potential depends upon his acceptance of his own finiteness.

The ultimate irony may be that there is no "truth" or "good" that justifies the denial of the quest for "truth" or "good," no "justice" that justifies even temporary injustice or cruelty. A liberation of the human spirit would make it possible to accept the realities of life and the realities of death of self and of others. In accepting these twin realities and in respecting the identity of others, we may give substance to the illusive human ego.

The human species in the nuclear age confronts a fundamental question: Can the species survive? It is becoming increasingly clear that ethical concerns once regarded as the province of theologians and philosophers have now become critical to human survival. Man's respect for his fellow man, abstractions like "decency," "justice," "equality," "compassion," "kindness," and "love" are the determinants of the continuance of human civilization.

An inability to define these new imperatives of human

survival and to transform these ethical "abstractions" into concrete and fundamental realities; an inability of individual human beings to free themselves from the more primitive demands of their constricted human egos and expand their egos to include sensitivity for the predicament of their fellow human beings; a pursuit of the goals of the past with the perspectives of the past and the methods of the past—these are the mocking, leering, cruel dilemmas of the human joke, through which the relentless human spirit may find the will to live.

PART

I

THE POWER
OF INTELLIGENCE
AND SURVIVAL

1

THE DUTY
OF
THE INTELLECTUAL

A TRADITIONAL AND PERVASIVE anti-intellectualism appears to characterize the American culture. At best, the intellectual in America is merely tolerated or mildly ridiculed; and at worst considered suspect or dangerous. So far he has not been systematically vilified or persecuted in America. The place of the intellectual in American culture has been determined by the dominant practical and pragmatic imperatives which have characterized American life.

The success of the American experiment of mass education and mass communication, paradoxically, contributes to the tenuousness of the status of the intellectual in American life. As a consequence of this demonstration of the validity of the democratic idea, standards of taste, value, and significance have become captives of the commercial market, determined by the judgment of the man in the street. A pragmatic approach to standards of value, consistent with a superficial concept of democracy, has determined that voting, counting, poll-taking, and profits are the ultimate

arbiters of worth. An unfinished task of our society—probably one that must be clearly identified, defined, and justified by intellectuals—is to learn to differentiate between
democratic philosophy, goals, and methods and stable standards of excellence. Literalistic egalitarianism, appropriate
and relevant to problems of political and social life, cannot
be permitted to invade and dominate the crucial areas of the
intellect, aesthetics, and ethics.

These and other considerations make any public discussion of the intellectual explicitly and implicitly awkward
and apologetic. In our culture the very term "intellectual"
appears to be a threatening term. It may even be considered
a snobbish term; and it certainly could be interpreted as an
egocentric term. It has been abused, distorted, and carica-
tured. It has been used as a basis for self-identification and
self-congratulation by the pompous, the empty, the lazy, by
the dilettante and the stuffed shirt. It has been used as a
mask for the moral and ethical equivocator and opportunist.
It has become a screen behind which the verbal liberal hides
when called to the confrontation that is consistent action.

The first requirement of a genuine intellectual is an obvious one. Not only must he be intelligent but he must respect
intelligence. He cannot apologize for or compromise with
the basic imperatives and difficulties involved in a life devoted to the creative use of human intelligence. An intellectual is a person who is compelled to think. He cannot stop
thinking even when the consequences of his thoughts would
be painful and lead him to unpopular conclusions. By some
perverse set of forces he is compelled to think critically. He
cannot accept prefabricated opinions. He cannot accept
opinions and ideas merely because they come from author-
ities, prestige figures, vested interests, established institu-

tions, sentiments, or loyalties. His primary if not exclusive loyalty must be the quest for truth—a truth uncontaminated, as far as possible, by the distortions of the human ego and its pretensions. The intellectual is caught in the imperatives of the Socratic observation that "the unexamined life is not worth living." To examine life critically and creatively requires courage, clarity, discipline, and compassion.

The intellectual demonstrates his courage by assuming the risk involved in the search for uncontaminated truth. He must risk the ridicule and repudiation of the masses. He must risk the attacks of the vested interests and controllers of power who fear the possibility that truth might be inimical to the maintenance of their own power. The ultimate courage required of the intellectual is the courage to face the essential aloneness and alienation that is his fate.

The clarity of the intellectual is in the first instance indicated by his awareness of the limitations of his role. He demonstrates that he has a socially useful perspective by the evidence of a clear and realistic perspective of self. No one who is confused about his own strengths and his own weaknesses can understand or help others. The clarity of the intellectual is also reflected by the clarity of his values. The quest for truth and justice would be meaningless without some guiding framework of accepted and acceptable values. These terms—truth and justice—have no meaning independent of a value system. If the intellectual is to be creatively effective and constructive, his contributions must be consistent with the Judeo-Christian axiom of the inherent worth and dignity of the individual human being. This is a limitation on his freedom of quest but it is an imperative one. Without it the intellectual would flounder in the swamp of sophistry and moral nihilism.

The discipline of the intellectual involves primarily that difficult training, control, and effort required to make the mind a creative instrument rather than a mere mirror or repository. Every intellectual must, therefore, be committed to gathering and evaluation of evidence and the determination of the appropriate, relevant, and logical conclusions. But the discipline of the intellectual is not only the discipline of his mind, it is a discipline of the total person. The most arduous aspect of discipline involves the control of one's own ego, one's biases, one's personal desires and the understandable and illusive personal wish for happiness and comfort, and related to this is the control of the arrogance of excessive and debilitating guilt or evasive and transparent humility.

The compassion of the intellectual is essential for understanding the universality of the human predicament. It is essential to the understanding of the inextricability of human frailty and strength, tragedy and comedy, reality and wish, rigidity and resilience, and pathos. This compassion is based upon empathy—the ability to see in one man all men; and in all men the self. The compassion of the intellectual should not be confused with sentimentality, however, for creative compassion does not free one of the demands of courage, intellectual and moral clarity, or discipline. The intellectual's role demands that his compassion provide substance and motivation to his commitment to think, to communicate, and to act forthrightly in the quest for truth and for justice.

The Marginal Outsider as Critical Intellectual

One of the characteristics of the intellectual is that he cannot be limited by color, nationality, creed, or any of the other arbitrary distinctions among men. In the case of the Negro intellectual in contemporary America his demands are the demands of the intellectual, only more so. This is the hard reality of being a Negro in America. Racism requires that the Negro bear the burdens and the trials and tribulations borne by others plus an extra burden which America so far has insisted upon placing upon an individual because of his color. This compound handicap will either toughen a critical small proportion of Negroes and demand of them the strength necessary to save America or it will destroy America.

There are increasing signs that white intellectuals in America are finding it more and more difficult to meet the severe standards required of the truly creative intellectual. Some have been silenced and intimidated. Some have been even more effectively suppressed through seduction by the Lorelei of success and status. Some have tried to continue the posture and verbalization of intellectualism without the required courage, integrity, and independence. Some have become apologists for the status quo under the guise of superpatriotism, intellectual sophistry, obscurantism, moral relativism, gradualism, moderation, pessimism, and cynicism. Some have become captives of one set of ideologies or another, changing the color of their thought to fit the changing postures of their ideological gods. And some have just given up in despair.

The ultimate irony of contemporary America is the fact that it might be imperative for the Negro to assume the decisive and difficult role of the critical intellectual if America is to be saved. If this role is inescapable for him and if he can assume it, this will be so precisely because the Negro has been excluded from full acceptance and participation in the apparent benefits and advantages of the American culture. From one perspective the rejection of all Negroes, without regard to intellectual potential or class distinctions, is an example of America's racist honesty. This is indeed democratic racism since all Negroes have been kept marginal and made aliens within their own land. It is a fact that marginality and alienation are required for that detached, penetrating, and realistic understanding of the forces operative in a culture. Those who are a part of, involved in, and seduced by their culture understandably will have difficulty in seeing and critically appraising the major stresses, strains, and forces which reflect either the capacity for growth or the stagnation and decadence of the culture.

In spite of racial exclusion, rejection, and stigma the Negro in America is an American. In spite of the present fashionable cult of Africanism, he is not an African. Nor is he a Moslem—no matter how attractive this escapist appeal might be to the excluded and the rejected. In spite of his protest and his just and insistent demands for unqualified equality as an American citizen, he is forced to recognize that his destiny is one with the destiny of America. If America does not survive, he cannot survive. He must therefore pray that there is still time within which the dangers inherent in wishful thinking, pompous bombast, outmoded status posturing, moral emptiness, hypocrisy, and equivocation can be corrected or ameliorated before they become fatal. If the Negro can provide through the creative use of some of his trained intelligence the necessary corrective to these destructive aspects of our society, then his three hundred years of suffering would not have been in vain. The urgent role of the Negro intellectual is to seek these correctives.

[24]

If the Negro is to help America regain its soul as a necessary condition to its survival, he can do so only under certain highly specific terms. The Negro intellectual must start from certain unquestioned premises: namely, the equality of man, the inhumanity of injustice, the right of every human being to contribute to the society of which he is a part the maximum of which he is capable and his freedom to do so without restrictions based on the irrelevance of race or color. These are elementary demands and imperatives of the complexity of our times. These imperatives are no longer arguable. The Negro intellectual can no longer afford to expend any significant proportion of his intellectual and emotional energies in the maelstrom of mere protest. He can no longer afford to waste his efforts in urgent pleas for acceptance of his humanity. We, the nation, and the world are beyond the point of compromise on these imperatives of democracy. We cannot partake of the moral hypocrisy and equivocation of gradualism, tokenism, and moderation. We cannot settle for the crumbs of justice. To do so would not only be intolerable to the intellect and deep emotions of the Negro, but what is probably more important, it would decrease markedly the chances of survival of western civilization. For the American Negro to compromise at this juncture of American and world history would make him an accessory to the disintegration of his own nation.

The task confronting the intelligent American Negro today is the awesome task of liberating white Americans from the moral corrosion of racism, rigidity, and wishful thinking so that our nation will have the strength to meet the terrifying challenges that must be faced and met. In demanding his rights and responsibilities, unqualified and uncompromised, the Negro affirms the inherent validity of the dignity of man.

He revitalizes the western European concept of the validity of man himself, and he asserts that the democratic idea is so powerful and so contagious that it cannot be restricted to a given group of men, a given color, a given nation, or a given region of the world. This is the meaning behind the freedom rides, the sit-ins, the quiet, persistent demand for political equality, and the other examples of the Negro's impatience with moral equivocation and procrastination.

As he seeks to interpret the more profound meaning of these indications of the emerging new and more effective image of the Negro, the Negro intellectual cannot become ensnared in or accept uncritically the oversimplifications or the strategic semantics of such terms as "love for the oppressor" or the frenetic hatred of the black supremacist. Neither of these positions—in spite of the fact that one seems acceptable to the tender conscience of many whites and the other seems terribly threatening to their guilt and fear—is compatible with the psychological realities or the social imperatives of the Negro's status and role in contemporary America. Nor can the Negro intellectual of today retreat to the conciliatory opportunism of Booker T. Washington or the quasi-snobbishness of early Du Bois.

The Negro must be free to criticize existing Negro leadership. Thus, paradoxically, the strength and success of the NAACP are reflected in the increasing critical appraisals of its philosophy and operations. Largely through the activities of the NAACP we are now secure enough and our morale is high enough to be self-critical. The criticism of the Negro intellectual must meet the test of constructiveness and must be geared to attempts to make the Negro organizations and leaders more adaptive and effective instruments of positive change. Like E. Franklin Frazier, he must be free to criticize the moral erosion and spiritual emptiness in his own group, even if occasionally his impatience and empathy seem to result in intemperance and lack of compassion.

The Negro intellectual must clearly differentiate his role from the equally important roles of others. He cannot confuse his role with that of the politician or the mass leader. He cannot hope to be successful by imitating or adopting their techniques or their slogans. He certainly cannot appeal to the man in the street through the uncritical use of slogans, emotional phrases, and other devices which have been found effective in arousing the emotions and allegiances of the crowd. On the contrary he is obligated to scrutinize the ideology, the motivation, and the methods of the popular leaders. He must interpret them and repudiate or accept them when the evidence so demands. The Negro intellectual would reduce his effectiveness if he sought to compete with others more competent and more suited in temperament and background for the status of popular leader. His role is to interpret, supplement, and give substance to the work of these leaders. He must content himself with the limited role of speaking to a minority at any given point in history. This, however, does not mean that the Negro intellectual can use this required division of labor as an excuse for withdrawal from social action. The dangers and imperatives of our times require that thought and responsible action merge into a single pattern of commitment.

The Negro writer and the artist who seek to interpret human suffering, courage, cruelty, desperation, and hope; the Negro physician who insists upon the highest standards of medical excellence and ethics as he serves his fellow man; the Negro lawyer who disciplines himself to present the cogent and relevant arguments for social justice; the

Negro teacher who involves himself completely in the paramount task of eliciting from each child the highest potential that is within him; the Negro worker who brings to his tasks the insatiable need for perfection; the Negro mother and father who place nothing above the need to transmit to their children an inviolable sense of their own worth and dignity as human beings, these exemplify the creative use of human intelligence. Each of these refutes the nuclear and self-fulfilling lie of American racism—the lie of the inferiority of the Negro.

To the extent that the Negro succeeds in freeing America from the shackles of trying to keep his people in an inferior position, the Negro will help America escape from the deadening mediocrity which now seems to ensnare it. It should now be clear that the Negro intellectual cannot acquiesce to the acceptance of the limited goals of racial integration. For him racial integration in America must mean more than the right of the Negro to share equally in the moral emptiness, hypocrisy, conformity, and despair that characterize so much of American life. To be truly meaningful, integration must provide the Negro with the opportunity, the right, and the obligation to contribute to our society a resurgence of ethical substance, moral strength, and general integrity. Specifically, the Negro can contribute to our society an ability to face and accept the fullness of life and the ability to dare the depths of love and enjoyment and even suffering and pain unafraid. In an integrated society the Negro can help to free our society from the tantalizing frustration that is its worship of materialism. The Negro can help our society to accept the totality that is man with minimum conflict, shame, guilt, or apology.

It is the fate of the Negro intellectual that he has no choice but to accept the challenge of trying to help America survive. He must exchange the dubious luxury of the life of quiet acquiescence and desperation for the freedom and risks involved in thinking, communicating, and reinforcing those ideas which are essential to America's survival. This is his commitment and obligation to himself, to his race, to his nation, and to his world. In the contemporary world these are indistinguishable.

2

SOCIAL MORALITY,
SCIENTIFIC OBJECTIVITY,
AND RELEVANCE

MAN IS AN ORGANISM that seeks and demands explanations. He has sought to understand the mysteries of his environment. He has asked questions, and searched for answers, about his origin and the meaning of his existence. He has been profoundly concerned and anxious about his ability to survive in the face of his comparative physical weaknesses and the multiple dangers of his environment. Man asks these questions and seeks their answers because he is an intelligent being who is not limited to mere behavioral interactions with his environment. He is a conscious, reflective, evaluative, anxious being who is required to be as responsive to the realities of his ideational and created environments as to his physical and biological environments. The fact of human intelligence demands this. Human intelligence also provides the key to the answers to the questions it is capable of raising. Man believes that he has survived as a species and will continue to survive in spite of his skeletal weakness because he has the intelligence necessary to probe, to seek to understand, and to control the environmental forces that threaten him.

So far, his experience supports this intellectual circularity and pervasive human chauvinism.

The critical question of this period of human history—the answer to which must also come from the critical use of man's mind—is whether or not human intelligence as traditionally defined offers any reliable assurance of human survival. This question may seem hopelessly abstract, even trite. But nothing could be more concrete. Is pure intelligence enough to protect man from self-inflicted destruction?

Paradox and irony are inherent in this question.

The choice is between a world of leisure, of productive and creative humanity, or a world destroyed through human intelligence. Man's understanding and his mastery of matter and energy justify his claims to God-like superiority, provide him with the basis for enriching and deepening human experience, and, at the same time, provide him with the instruments for ultimate destruction.

Science and technology, among the constructive benefits of human intelligence, cannot, at present, be divorced from possible destructive or inhuman uses. Modern man has placed his intelligence disproportionately at the service of the masters of power, technology, and war at the expense of an understanding of those forces which constitute man himself and the nature of his relations with his fellow man. Some have sought to resolve this dilemma by suggesting that certain scientific discoveries be destroyed or blocked before fulfillment. Yet the power of thought cannot be artificially or arbitrarily controlled without atrophy. We cannot have the benefits of the unfettered mind without freedom and risk. To control intelligence in the attempt to ensure only benevolent

[31]

consequences would be a Pyrrhic victory sentencing the human race to ignorance, stagnation, and decadence. It would probably also be impossible.

Free human intelligence and its richest consequences—science, technology, art, literature, philosophy, and religion —are essential to human progress and survival. But in their pure form they are not enough. They do not in themselves reduce the capricious dangers and hazards to life. They bring with them now the novel and awesome possibility of self-inflicted annihilation.

We claim to understand all that we need to know about the structure of the atom—how to release at least some of its vast store of energy. With this knowledge we promise and we threaten, we alternately strut with arrogance and cower in fear, we boast and we implore, we hope for a fuller life and we despair that we might die. We point with justified pride to our conquest of plagues and diseases. Each new victory establishes the strategy for the defeat of still another microscopic enemy of human life. We have made discoveries and developed techniques that would result in the production of food for a world's population much greater than that which now exists. We could, if we dared, laugh at the constricted pessimism of the Malthusians.

Now our gods are the gods of Intelligence, Science, and Technology. These gods have their powerful priests and apostles. Their true believers are uncritically abject, obsequious, and worshipful in the faith that these omnipotent and omniscient gods will protect and save them and enrich their lives. But there remains the gnawing suspicion that these contemporary gods are fickle and treacherous. They promise and they taunt. They fulfill and they tantalize. They offer the extension and the deepening of life and they threaten imminent extinction. They play with man as they dare him to question their power. They know that man dares not doubt, dares not question, and dares not now reject them because to do so would be to throw him back to a state of futility, helplessness, insecurity, and despair even more stultifying than that faced by his most primitive ancestors. Man now emerges as the victorious prisoner of his own intelligence. He cowers in each victory. As he rockets to the moon, he plans the futility of protection from nuclear devastation on earth.

In this nuclear and space age when the arrogance of man seems close to realization, it has become increasingly clear that superior human intelligence, narrowly defined as the ability to manipulate ideas and things, does not guarantee human survival. In fact, the intelligence measurable by psychologists is the gravest threat to the survival of the human species. The extinction of life on this earth can now be achieved through the effort of constricted, segmentalized, isolated genius. This is no longer a figment of the overactive imagination of science fiction writers, but the overriding anxiety of our times. Before this monster, his own creation, man seems paralyzed by a silently pervasive panic.

Panic is nonadaptive. The individual in a state of panic tends to act irrationally, without regard to the level of his intelligence. He is either immobile or he engages in actions contrary to survival demands. He becomes rigid, adhering to a single pattern or direction of behavior in spite of persistent evidence that the effort does not lead to the desired solution. His weaknesses are intensified and his strengths obscured. His rational, intellectual powers are suspended and he seems dominated by deep and terrifying atavistic forces. The terror of these forces is no less if the panic is cold and unemotional,

[33]

or emotional and explosive. This terror appears to be greater when the panic is a contagiously collective or group phenomenon. These conditions of panic seem to apply to our contemporary world. Man is confronted with what appears to be the ultimate paradox. He must save himself, if he is to be saved, by the same resource that has threatened his survival. Human intelligence must plan for survival. It must find new capacities within itself. An intelligence of aloof unconcern has no adaptive or meaningful value at this time. Whatever might have been its historical significance or justification, the pretense that the scholar, the intellectual, or the scientist could or should remain apart from the day-to-day problems of lesser men is no longer tenable. The German concentration camps and atomic bomb attacks on a civilian population introduced a period of collective guilt, collective panic, and shared responsibility for resolution. The man of intellect cannot divorce himself from this new society. He cannot pretend that these crucial decisions must be made either by the masses or the elite of power. Ironically, it was a high type of human intellect that precipitated our contemporary panic and guilt, but the liberation of energy from the nucleus of the atom was a feat of a limited component or compartment of human intelligence. The liberation of mankind from the impending doom inherent in an age of ultimate destructive weaponry existing in the context of the persistence of human cruelty and injustice must come from the totality of human intelligence.

This paradox of human intelligence can be resolved only through the use of courageous and creative human intelligence. A reasonable starting postulate could be that the present threats to survival do not result from too much intelligence, or too much science, or even from too much technology. Like his ancestors who faced crises of survival, contemporary man is also threatened by ignorance. In spite of all of the things that we know—or believe that we know; in spite of our tremendous technology, our gadgets, our battleships, our airplanes, our electronic transporters, communicators, calculators—we are today faced with a powerful and mocking core of ignorance. We are ignorant of ourselves. We are ignorant of the nature of man. We have little or no understanding of the nature of human love, kindness, hatred, greed, avarice, empathy, lust for power, conformity, and the other powerful stresses and currents that constitute the human ego. Man must meet these newly recognized mysteries exactly as he met the other mysteries that he believed threatened his survival by using his intelligence to understand and thereby to attempt to control them. The imbalance between the advances in physical science and technology and the retardation in social and psychological sciences and morality, like past forms of major imbalances, poses a survival quandary for man. We cannot delay—time no longer is unlimited. The ignorance of modern man, however, is not that which can be cured by the exercise of pure intelligence. His critical ignorance lies in an inadequate functional sense of social morality.

Many nuclear physicists and other scientists have given evidence of their deep concern for the future of man. The social and political activities of Albert Einstein, the social action and protests of Bertrand Russell and Linus Pauling are merely a few examples of this type of commitment to the survival of mankind. Nonetheless, too few men of intellectual stature in other fields of science, humanities, literature, and religion have had the courage or dare to raise their voices in a mobilized effort to save mankind from its confused emotional and intellectual perversity.

Intelligence, to be effective and functional, must be freed from petty provincialisms of race, nationality, language, creed, religion, or region that constrict human perception. The destiny of any group of human beings is linked to the destiny of all human beings. No solution to the contemporary crisis will work for some human beings if it is denied to others.

Effective human intelligence must be free from the need to purchase acceptability and status from any given group of men with the high price of compliance, conformity, affability, and obsequious deference to the prevailing interests and power groups. Effective and functional intelligence cannot withdraw or seek safety within ivory towers. It cannot deny validity or turn away from the real, the difficult, and the painful problems of men. Courage and intelligence are now inseparable.

The more complex, creative, and moral components of intelligence have not, and probably cannot be reduced to the level of the relatively simple techniques of measurement so far devised by psychologists. They cannot evaluate human dignity and worth. They do not determine whether superior human intelligence will be used as a social trust for the benefit of mankind or for personal gain, aggrandizement, or expediency.

A unidimensional intelligence concerned only with ideas in the abstract or with mere demonstrable utility could assert that the work of intelligent men should be amoral, nonevaluative, detached, and harnessed to an impersonal, if not inhuman, science and technology. The problems produced by such monster-creating atavistic intelligence can only be resolved by a multidimensional and complex intelligence. It must be an intelligence of moral commitment complicated and pervaded by an inescapable human and social concern. It must be free, yet disciplined by respect for the dignity and the beauty of order, of truth, and of justice. It must understand that man's search for survival, status, and meaning can succeed only within a stable, ethical society. Without such dimension, human intelligence remains paradoxically the greatest danger to human survival.

Social morality is illusive and difficult to define. It involves not only man's intelligence but his feelings and his total being.

It depends upon man's capacity to give and to receive love, to be kind and to be empathic. Love in its most concrete sense is a primary emotion essential to the preservation of the species. It is a positive and adaptive emotion, which involves an affinity and desire for closeness with another human being. Kindness may be viewed as the generalized expression of love, concern, and sensitivity in interpersonal relations, empathy as the ability to feel into and to identify with the needs of another human being. An empathic person shares another's concerns, joys, anguish, despair, frustrations, hopes, and aspirations as if they were his own. Empathy, unlike love, is not concrete and primary but requires the capacity for abstract thought. Empathy is not possible for a limited, defective, egocentric, or animalistic human organism. Without empathy, neither social morality nor responsibility, neither justice nor human society itself would be possible. In empathy, human intelligence, love, and kindness converge.

There are so-called tough-minded realists who contend

that love, kindness, and empathy are mere disguises for more powerful and primitive egocentric and animalistic impulses in man. They contend that there is no stable basis for social morality, and that all morality is a thin pretensive veneer quick to disappear under stress, deprivation, or adversity. This debate between the advocates of man's moral capacity and obligations and those who contend that only egocentric power imperatives are important has dominated man's struggle to define the dimensions of his humanity from the awakening of human consciousness up to the Vietnam protests.

The Moral Default of Education

Those who argue that man is incapable of achieving a dependable form of social morality have written an epitaph to the human species. Probably the only protection for contemporary man is to discover how to use his intelligence in the service of love and kindness. Some way must be found in the training of human beings to instill moral sensitivity as an integral part of the complex pattern of functional human intelligence, to give human beings the assurance to love, the security to be kind, and the integrity required for a functional empathy.

Traditionally, the realm of social morality was left to religion and the churches as guardians or custodians, but they failed to fulfill this responsibility and yielded to the seductive lures of wealth and pomp. The "God is Dead" rhetoric was the result. For the more pragmatic men of power simplistic Machiavellianism must remain the guiding principle of their decisions—power *is* morality, morality is power.

[38]

The task of producing human beings with trained morally sensitive intelligence must be assumed by educators, though the task will be no easier for our colleges and universities than it has been for our churches—our universities are a part of a society dominated by power. They too seek the protection, safety, and status that come with identification with those who have power.

Education has many subtle forms of escape from social and moral responsibility, among them the postures and assertions of moral relativism, of academic detachment, of philosophical purity, and of scientific objectivity. The moral relativists say right and wrong, good and bad, justice and injustice are relative values not subject to empirical, objective, or consistent definition. They assert that moral values are determined by the society or culture in which the individual is socialized and that the prevailing social norms will determine what a person believes and how he behaves toward his fellow man. This view, arising from the important work of the cultural anthropologists, reflected the growing liberalism and tolerance of human differences characteristic of certain aspects of twentieth-century American social science. But the fashionable oversimplification of moral relativism and its confusion with moral nihilism masked the basic fact that man is unique as a value-seeking and moral organism. The horrors of infanticide, genocide, and Hitlerian Nazism cannot be comprehended or dealt with within moral relativism's limited and naïve conceptual framework. Literalistic moral relativism must be seen as indifference, as insensitivity, and as moral and intellectual confusion. To the extent that colleges and universities promulgate this point of view without powerful countervailing probes, they provide an adequate escape from any moral commitment for themselves and they leave their students without moral guidelines essential for the responsible use of intelligence.

The same must be said for the postures of academic detachment and scientific objectivity when they preclude the making of moral judgments and entail the rejection of the responsibility to remedy what is wrong or unjust in our society. It is argued that detachment and objectivity are required for the discovery of truth. But what is the value of a soulless truth? Does not truth require meaning? And does not meaning require a context of values? Is there any meaningful or relevant truth without commitment?

How is it possible to study a slum objectively? What kind of human being can remain detached as he watches the dehumanization of other human beings? Why would one want to study a sick child except to make that child well?

Intellectual detachment and scientific objectivity can be insidious and dangerous forms of moral irresponsibility. Indifference, equivocation, and expediency avoid the risks engendered by the use of human intelligence for the attainment of social justice and human progress. When our colleges and universities become havens from value, when our teachers become defenders of such transparent escapes, they abdicate their responsibilities for moral leadership and they contribute to, if not help to create, the profound tragedy of the moral erosion and emptiness of those who have the intellectual gifts that might make human advancement and survival possible.

The persistent protests of a small number of our college students extensively reported in the newspapers beginning with the first sit-ins of Negro college students, followed by the Berkeley rebellion and the Vietnam protests, can be seen as symptomatic of the deep undercurrent of moral uneasiness of sensitive young people. They are demanding of their colleges and the universities some demonstration of humanity. They are demanding honesty. They are demanding evidence of concern with justice. They are demanding that colleges and universities be socially and morally relevant. They are few, and they are anguished and confused; but they are concerned—and they assume the risks of the concerned.

So far our colleges and universities and the men who control and run them have not yet answered these young people affirmatively. Perhaps they do not understand them. It is probable that the years of moral denial and studied blindness to flagrant problems of social injustice that were deemed essential to the efficient financing and administration of a large and complex educational institution have made it difficult and impractical to listen to pleas for dialogue and for resolution of fundamental moral issues. Our colleges and universities have a long history of default on important moral issues. They have frequently tried to make a virtue of isolation from the problems of the marketplace and from the anguished yearnings of the deprived and powerless people of our society. They have thrown in their lot with the powerful in government, business, and industry. Their concern with purity of research is reconciled with relative ease as they accept larger and larger grants and subsidies from the Defense Department, from the CIA, and from big business for work on practical problems—problems of power. It is only when the issue is directly or indirectly one of social justice or fundamental social change that our colleges and universities raise questions about the propriety of institutional involvement or the role of a professor and ask whether involvement is consistent with the pure and detached quest for truth.

Probably the chief exception to these severe charges would be found in the research and teaching in the medical and public health schools of our universities, which are directly tied to human need and human welfare. Their findings must be directly or indirectly relevant. They cannot be pompously trivial. But even they are more concerned with individual cure than with the prevention of the conditions of poverty and degradation that lead to disease.

There are many specific and relevant areas in which American colleges and universities have defaulted in providing morally sensitive intellectual leadership for our society:

- They have watched silently and facilitated the process of ruthless competition in education from the primary grades on. In such a process the possibility of empathy, concern for one's colleague, and the use of superior intelligence as a social trust are precluded; our children learn from the demands of their teachers and the insistence of their parents that education is competition and that intelligence is a device to obtain superior status and economic advantage over others.

- Under the guise of efficiency and at the price of reflective and critical thought, the demands of mass education and the pressure of limited facilities in our colleges have helped reduce the educational process to the level of content retention required for the necessary score on the College Boards and the Graduate Record Examinations.

- They have permitted our elementary and secondary schools to become contaminated by and organized in terms of the educationally irrelevant factors of race and economic status.

- They have watched without sustained protests the erosion of the quality of education provided for minority-group children and other lower-status children—erosion to the point of criminal inefficiency and dehumanization.
- They have watched in silence the creeping blight of our cities and the spawning of Negro ghettos, concerned only when the pathologies associated with the ghetto come too close to the walls of the university. Only then do they seek to protect themselves, sometimes through a ruthless and callous dispossessing of the unwanted lower-status people.
- They have abdicated any sustained, forthright moral leadership in America's attempt to resolve the anguish of its pervasive racial problem. Leadership in the civil rights struggle has come instead from civil rights organizations, from the federal courts, and, later, from the executive and legislative branches of the federal and some state governments; and from the Catholic, Protestant, and Jewish churches and synagogues. Despite the commitment of some of their faculty, American colleges and universities have, as institutions, remained detached and nonrelevant to this major domestic issue of our times. Indeed, colleges and universities are major bastions of a subtle and persistent form of white supremacy.

Given the persistence and deification of the detached definition of scholarship and the purposes of education, it is easy to understand how some observers, within and outside the academic community, could look upon colleges and universities as indifferent, insensitive, and even cruel. These institutions have prided themselves on their pursuit of truth and beauty in the face of the flagrant injustices, ignorance, and filth that afflicted the masses of their fellow human beings.

Our institutions of higher education, even in allegedly democratic America, have as their models feudal, isolated baronies. Some resemble fastnesses, within whose walls only would-be intellectual, social, and economic aristocrats are permitted to enter and partake of the feast of scholarly detachment. The goals and purposes of colleges and universities can no longer be defined in terms of an elitist, snobbish preparation of a few for a specialized role as clergyman, scholar, or economic or governmental potentate. The days when education, and particularly higher education, could be perceived, organized, and governed as if it were a luxury to be reserved for the privileged, or for those who aspired to the status of advantaged desperation, have abruptly ended. But little warning was given to the educational institutions, whose assumptions, goals, practices, and governing structures have suddenly become archaic.

The first significant breach in the walls of educational elitism came in the early twentieth century as American colleges and universities, particularly the public and land grant colleges, became more effective social instruments in facilitating the upward economic mobility of the children of working class and immigrant groups. But my biased perspective tells me that this initial victory did not lead to total victory, did not result in hordes of the underprivileged breaking through or storming the walls of the citadels of learning. The rather formidable barriers of the traditional have remained—the aura of snobbish intellectual elitism, the insensitivity, the egocentricity, the loss of memory of those of the formerly deprived, who themselves benefited from the limited democratization of higher education, and became intense adversaries and agents of exclusion of the presently deprived.

To remove these remaining barriers is now the obligation of colleges and universities—if they are to survive, and if they are to help a democratic society to survive. It will not be easy to complete the job of democratizing American education and at the same time to maintain and increase the integrity and validity of education, to conserve, train, discipline, and, above all, increase the supply of the precious resource of human intelligence. But this must be done.

Colleges and universities that are serious in undertaking this most difficult task must resist all temptations to engage in gimmickry, in superficial, flamboyant, and "public relations" charades. Serious programs must be planned carefully and pursued vigilantly and with the flexibility that differentiates blind dogmatism from a respect for experience and evidence. As a social psychologist, I am aware that institutions and bureaucracies do not change easily; and, for reasons at present not clearly understood but I believe inherently perverse, educational institutions seem particularly resistant to change. But they must change if they are to survive.

The fundamental structure, authority, and prestige patterns of higher educational institutions have been challenged irrevocably. Amid the babel of sometimes silly student protests, some probing questions have been asked by a critical minority of the present generation of students about the purposes, the function, and therefore, inevitably, the governance of our universities. They must be answered, not just in words or rationalization, but by demonstrations of increased efficiency and social sensitivity. This is not to say that all of the suggestions and demands for changes in the policies and governance of colleges and universities will lead to adaptive and more constructive roles for these institutions. Some of these demands, particularly the nonnegotiable ones, are on their face frivolous or perverse. I do not believe, for example, that students should be permitted to determine the nature or substance of the curricula. I do not see that this would in itself ensure "relevance" or sensitivity. If students were competent to play such a role seriously, then they should not be students. If students knew before embarking on the challenging and exciting path of seeking an education what was and what was not relevant—what should and should not be read or discussed—then they would have demonstrated either a level of *a priori* genius that would make education unnecessary or a closed-minded dogmatism that would make education impossible.

I do believe, however, that the demand by some students for a radical reformation of admissions policies is a serious, adaptive, and constructive contribution to the eventual reorganization and democratization and, therefore, increased effectiveness of our colleges and universities. Such programs must contribute additional dimensions of depth, quality, and a sense of man's responsibility for his fellow man. The programs cannot be administered in ways that intensify superficial differences among human beings; they cannot be condescending or sentimental or guilt-laden. They must be designed so that the academic competence of previously educationally disadvantaged students will be increased and so that the intellectual and empathic needs of all students will be mobilized and channeled. Above all, such a program would add an important and now missing dimension to contemporary higher education, infusing into the educational

[46]

process the sense of social responsibility, the obligation of human beings to use superior human intelligence and economic and educational advantages as a social trust—empathically—rather than as competitive weapons that encourage cheating and superficiality among even our better students. This dimension of social responsibility I believe to be the chief determinant of whether human intelligence and education are to be dangerously and incredibly destructive or whether intelligence and education will provide the means to build more just and rational societies worthy of man.

Special programs must be developed to help white students from less privileged backgrounds and from more privileged affluent families grow beyond the constricted racist view of their parents and peers. Colleges and universities must assume the specific task of educating these young people so that they will be free of such moral and ethical disadvantage. The survival of our cities—certainly our development of communities worthy of man—might depend as much upon educational programs for disadvantaged whites as upon programs of educational opportunities for disadvantaged minorities.

Ethically neglected and glutted by insensitive affluence, young economically privileged whites have been the victims of indifference disguised as permissiveness, robbed of a sense of identity and personal worth and integrity by the moral equivocation and inconsistencies of their successful parents and peers. These young people have been crying for help. In their desperation they have imitated the outward symbols of dress, speech, and music of the most deprived segment of our society, the blacks, and they have been ignored and at times stigmatized or beaten as if they were black.

[47]

A sensitive minority of American youth—college students and ghetto casualties—are urgently trying to tell us that equivocation in the face of flagrant or subtle social injustices is no longer tolerable. A positive sense of their own being and human worth is eroded by a cloying, spiritually empty affluence and by remediable deprivation. Drugs and cults and romantic escapes into hedonism and even justifiable and random rage will not be enough to ease their unrest. Their anguished and at times seemingly incoherent cries have the basic coherence of insisting that the demands for colleges that are adaptive and the demands for cities worthy of the grandeur of man are basically the same.

Our colleges must help our cities become symbols of respect for man and concrete monuments of the inviolable sense of human dignity. Our colleges must transfer the monies, the brains, and the prestige previously associated with space and war research to research on how man can live in peace and justice with his fellow man, how the urban environment can be transformed into beauty and tranquillity, and how the masses of human beings can come to understand that love and kindness and justice and empathy are the necessary parameters of human intelligence and the imperatives of social stability and the survival of the human species.

The major charge that must now be made against American colleges and universities is that they have not fulfilled their responsibility and obligation to develop and train human beings with a morally relevant and socially responsible intelligence. They have operated as if it were possible for a detached, amoral intelligence to be adaptive. They have not provided their students with the moral guidelines essential for the effective, creative, and adaptive use of superior intelligence. They have not provided their faculties with the stimulation or protection for a socially responsible use of their own critical intelligence. And above all they have not provided the moral leadership for society—they have not alerted the public to the urgency of finding moral and democratic solutions to critical domestic and international problems.

American higher education need not continue to subordinate itself to the goals of efficiency, expediency, power, status, and success. Young people can be trained in our schools, colleges, and universities to value critical and independent thought above affability; to value individuality and creativity above conformity and packaged opinions; to value evidence of concern, commitment, and social sensitivity above personal acceptance and mere social success.

A realistic basis for hope is man's capacity for empathy. Man struggles for values. He insists and argues and demands and dies and kills in his tortuous and often pathetic quests for moral stabilities. Empathy, like intelligence, can be made more functional and effective through education. If it is trained and directed it can become meaningful for the individual and adaptive for the society. If it is untrained it becomes unpredictable, random, or misdirected, or it atrophies. The acceptance of the responsibility to reinforce man's empathic capacity as an integral part of the responsibility to train intellect is now the clear challenge of relevance confronting contemporary educational institutions.

A truly educated person is trained to mesh his intelligence with his feelings in a disciplined whole. He cannot deny or subordinate either his brain or his heart, because each is essential to the effective functioning of the other. Our colleges must provide the opportunities for students to test

[49]

their courage to stand alone—to accept the risks of alienation and aloneness that come with the anguish and the
torture of the search for moral commitment and disciplined,
intelligent action. Colleges must be the place where human
beings are prepared to bolster intelligence with compassion,
courage, and increasing wisdom. American colleges and universities will demonstrate that they are relevant to the
crucial issues of our times, that they are morally adaptive,
and therefore that they can contribute to the survival of the
human race, when they fully and functionally accept as their
responsibility the need to train individuals of moral intelligence. Such individuals would demonstrate by the totality of
their lives that they understand that an injustice perpetrated
upon any human being robs them of some of their humanity
and demands of them personal, constructive, and intelligent
action for justice. Human intelligence tempered by wisdom
and moral sensitivity is not now an ethical abstraction. It
is a survival imperative. Education that is genuinely relevant—even for physicians, businessmen, lawyers, and engineers—must make room for and encourage the spontaneous
and the creative intelligence that cannot be bound by institutional conformity. It must do so even for pragmatic reasons, for no institution survives without dependency on—
without exploitation of—the creative mind. So, too, social
science cannot be relevant if it surrenders to rigidities; it,
too, must depend on the insight and the empathy of the free
spirit.

The Limits of Relevance

As one who began himself to use the term "relevant" and
to insist on its primacy years ago, I feel an obligation to

protest the limits of relevance or to propose a redefinition of it to embrace wider terms.

Definitions of education that depend on immediate relevance ignore a small but critical percentage of human beings, the individuals who for some perverse reason are in search of an education that is not dominated by the important, socially and economically required pragmatic needs of a capitalist or a communist or a socialist society. Such an individual is not certain what he wants to be; he may not even be sure that he wants to be successful. He may be burdened with that perverse intelligence that finds the excitement of life in a continuous involvement with ideas.

For this student, education may be a lonely and tortuous process not definable in terms of the limits of course requirements or of departmental boundaries, or the four- or six-year span of time required for the bachelor's or graduate degree. This student seems unable to seek or to define or to discuss relevance in terms of externals. He seems somehow trapped by the need to seek the dimensions of relevance in relation to an examination and re-examination of his own internal values. He may have no choice but to assume the burden of seeking to define the relevance of the human experience as a reflection of the validity of his own existence as a value-seeking, socially sensitive, and responsive human being. He is required to deny himself the protective, supporting crutch of accepting and clutching uncritically the prevailing dogmatisms, slogans, and intellectual fashions.

If such a human being is to survive the inherent and probably inevitable aloneness of intellectual integrity, he must balance it by the courage to face and accept the risks of his individuality; by compassion and empathetic identification with the frailties of his fellow human beings as a reflection

[51]

of his own; by an intellectual and personal discipline which prevents him from wallowing in introspective amorphousness and childlike self-indulgence. And, certainly, he must demonstrate the breadth of perspective and human sensitivity and depth of affirmation inherent in the sense of humor which does not laugh at others but laughs with man and with the God of Paradox who inflicted upon man the perpetual practical joke of the human predicament.

American colleges, with few notable exceptions, provide little room for this type of student, just as American society provides little room for such citizens. Perhaps it is enough to see that institutions of higher education do not destroy such potential. One could hope wistfully that our colleges and even our multiuniversities could spare space and facilities to serve and to protect those students who want to experiment without being required to be practical, pragmatic, or even relevant.

Is it still possible within the complexity and cacophony of our dynamic, power-related, and tentatively socially sensitive institutions for some few to have the opportunity to look within, to read, to think critically, to communicate, to make mistakes, to seek validity, and to accept and enjoy this process as valid in itself? Is there still some place where relevance can be defined in terms of the quest—where respect for self and others can be taken for granted as one admits not knowing and is therefore challenged to seek?

May one dare to hope for a definition of education which makes it possible for man to accept the totality of his humanity without embarrassment? This would be valuable for its own sake, but it might also paradoxically be the most pragmatic form of education—because it is from these perverse, alone-educated persons that a practical society receives antidotes to a terrifying sense of inner emptiness and despair. They are the font of the continued quest for meaning in the face of the mocking chorus of meaninglessness. They offer the saving reaffirmation of stabilizing values in place of the acceptance of the disintegration inherent in valuelessness. They provide the basis for faith in humanity and life rather than surrender to dehumanization and destruction. From these impracticals come our poets, our artists, our novelists, our satirists, our humorists. They are our models of the positives, the potentials, the awe and wonder of man. They make the life of the thinking human being more endurable and the thought of a future tolerable.

PART

II

SOCIAL SCIENCE
AND
SOCIAL POWER

3

THE SCIENCE
OF
HUMAN MORALITY

MAN'S SUCCESSIVE VICTORIES over ignorance and superstition have postponed the probability that the physical environment will destroy him. But he now confronts the reality that the seeds of destruction are inherent in the fruits of knowledge.

This is the significant dilemma of modern man: to control social and psychological forces is as essential to his survival as control of the forces of the physical universe. To fail in this will be a prelude to tragedy. Each new development in science has negative as well as positive potentialities, but the consequences of human conflicts and social tensions become increasingly catastrophic as man gains mastery over his physical universe.

The technological achievement of transforming matter into energy through atomic fission is, for man, the absolute realization of the paradox. Atomic fission offers a challenge and a hope, but it is an instrument of ultimate destruction, filling man's heart and mind with guilt and terror.

[57]

Which alternative will dominate cannot be determined by amoral physical science itself. Science will not limit itself or deliberately retard its progress or destroy its findings. The question whether the destructive or constructive potentials will dominate must be answered not by less science, but by more.

The major threat to the stability and security of human society in the contemporary world is the marked discrepancy between the achievements of physical science and technology and the retardation in the development of the social sciences. It is imperative that the social sciences now develop the same objectivity and exactness most modern physical science has achieved.

A truly scientific social science will seek to understand the processes of social and individual interaction—the nature and dynamics of social relations—so it can reach a more valid prediction and control of social phenomena and, at the same time, conserve the dignity and integrity of individual personality. Inherent in this basic goal is the assumption that social stability is meaningless—if not impossible—independent of the stability and dignity of human beings. An asserted dichotomy between social stability and individual security would be clearly incompatible with meaningful social science.

The social and psychological sciences must be determined by a tough-minded search for facts, free from prejudice and stultifying preconceptions. The social scientist must be free to search for his facts unfettered by the biases of myths, mysticism, and the pleadings of special privilege, guided only by his own intelligence and integrity and a dedication to the search for truth. A socially realistic social science would recognize, however, that the quest for fact and truth of social phenomena, unlike the quest in the physical sciences, cannot proceed on the premise of the basic amorality of scientific fact. Fact in the physical universe seems to be empirically amoral, but, precisely, therefore, discoveries of such fact appear to man as two-headed monsters, capable of either destructive or constructive use. A scientific social science can lead to constructive technological advances only as it works within a stable and moral conceptual framework. To be "constructive," "socially desirable," and "beneficial" is, inescapably, to be moral.

Instead of seeking to ape the physical sciences in an assumption of amorality the social sciences may be forced to recognize that they are essentially the sciences of human morality. They can contribute to human social stability; they can counter the threat inherent in advance in the physical sciences.

A scientific exploitation of social phenomena would require analysis of social tensions and a determination of their causes. Some relevant questions to be answered are these:

What is the relationship between social tension and individual adjustment?

What forms of social tension most influence personal adjustment?

Through what media do social tensions impinge upon the individual and influence his adjustment?

What are the effects of personal motivations and the characteristics of the individual on the structure and stability of society?

In what ways, if any, are intergroup conflicts, international crises, and wars understandable in terms of disturbances in the personalities of specific individuals—for example, leaders— or in terms of characteristics common to many?

Such questions imply a set of moral values and principles, whether articulated or inarticulate. The terms "social tension" and "individual adjustment" would, indeed, be meaningless except in reference to a basic sense of values that suggests that social stability is a positive state of society and social tension a negative one. But, by what processes does stability deteriorate into tension? Stability in itself may be a symptom of social stagnation and potential decadence. If so, social tension would be seen in a more positive light as a symptom of the dynamics of social change and as an inevitable factor in social progress. The biological concepts of emergent evolution provide some support for this speculation. The common view that mere stability is a positive state of society and tension a negative symptom must, in consequence, be re-examined. The apparent antithesis may be reconciled by differentiating static stability from dynamic stability, one an index of stagnation and decadence, the other a necessary condition for positive development of the society. Conflicts, potential violence, and eventual extinction threaten a society in stasis, but the tensions in a society of dynamic stability would be symptomatic of positive change and progress.

A socially responsible social science would, then, be required to determine how to channelize social tensions to support dynamic growth and stability and how to prevent undirected tensions from reaching the critical point of frustration and deterioration. Social tension results in and is itself a consequence of profound individual needs and frustrations. This cyclic relationship tends to reinforce itself until a critical point when a pattern of friction, conflict, or spasmodic violent aggressions emerges.

Social stability may reflect balance within the social organism or the equilibrium of potential competing forces. Social tension may begin as pre-violent conflict and competition for priority in the satisfaction of needs. It may be seen as a state of disequilibrium, with competing forces struggling for additional power or dominance, threatening an increase in frustration of others and disturbing the functional equilibrium of the social organism.

A scientific study of social tensions would not only explore the statics and dynamics of the power structure within a society, but also—what seems to be even more fundamental —the psychology of human motivation. A logical and systematic transition into more empirical research on the problem would be to determine the objective indices of detrimental tension. In the more overt symptoms of social disorganization already recognized, in the family, in the community, the nation, and the international community, social scientists may find a place to begin. For example:

1. The instability of family relations, reflected in divorce rates, abandonment statistics, and child-welfare problems, seems related to social tensions.

2. Crime, juvenile delinquency, neuroses, and psychoses may be manifestations of disintegration of the personality that result from, among other causes, the bombardment of social pressures upon the individual.

3. Intergroup conflicts, such as racial and religious friction, labor-management problems, intense political conflicts, seem to be well recognized as symptoms of basic pathology or emergent social changes. But, whether such conflicts are symptoms of deterioration or of eventual positive change

may be related to the nature and structure of the society as a whole. Their existence in a society marked by striking, crystallized differences in privileges among social, economic, and political groups—approaching the rigidity of a caste system—suggests pathology. It is a reasonable assumption that social tensions reflect profound systemic disturbance and not imminent positive social change when some in a society have more than enough to satisfy their basic material needs and needs for status and prestige while others lack even the minimal requirements of human living.

4. Chronic competitions for power internationally also indicate a fundamental and increasingly significant social tension. If such crises are permitted to develop lawlessly, without control, they will end inevitably in the catastrophe of war, the most dramatic manifestation of man's ignorance of, and inability to control, those psychological and social forces that threaten his existence.

Understanding of the nature of tensions does not, however, provide an understanding of their dynamics or their genesis, yet such understanding is probably necessary to resolution. Social scientists must relate what they have learned in one field to what they know in another if the origin and nature of social tensions are to be understood.

Are the dynamics of social stability and social tensions related to principles that have primary relevance to the motivation and adjustment of the individual?

Attempts to understand and interpret social phenomena in terms of individual motivation did increase after the rise of Fascism, an unmistakable manifestation of the pathological potentials of human society. Although the struggle and competition for national or international power may not be explained wholly and simply as analogous to the power drive in personal relations, the personal may provide significant insights into the political.

Social psychologists no longer find a dichotomy between the individual and the group tenable as a significant hypothesis. Sufficient evidence is available to suggest a basic similarity in the dynamics of each. The transition from individual adjustment and interpersonal relations to an understanding of social interaction and the nature of social tension is not possible or fruitful on a simple linear level. A difference in degree exists, but the same basic principles may work, nevertheless, in a simple or more complex configurational pattern.

The social scientist's next job is to engage in pure research in the problems of human behavior. Social science has, for example, minimal reliable information on the characteristics of leaders and their effect on the stability of society, yet leaders are capable of exerting tremendous power. The existence of millions is immediately affected by their judgment. Given this obvious fact, the tremendous ignorance of leadership behavior is shocking. We have no objective information on such simple dimensions as the criteria of maturity of personality and intellect required for stable leadership. We do not even know whether or not some of the facets of personality structure which are important in achieving leadership are detrimental to social stability. It could be possible that an individual can become a leader only if he is insensitive to certain realities on which social stability itself depends. Lack of knowledge on such a problem seems no longer tolerable. For psychiatrists, psychologists, and others

[63]

interested in society and stability, this would seem a key immediate problem.

It is crucial also for social science to study the degree of impact of social forces on the personality, on the nature of motives, their genesis, their control, the degree to which similar patterns of disturbances in personal motivation in large numbers of people in turn determine social processes and social tensions. It is not enough to generalize on these problems; if the social sciences are to achieve their goal of control, it is important to determine such questions with exactness. One would want to know the specific relationships among these factors:

1. Minority status and personal values and attitudes. What is the effect of the socially accepted dehumanization of the individual on his attitudes toward the stability of the overall society? How does his personal attitude toward the society that debases him affect the stability of that society?

2. The effect of overt social tensions such as wars on the emerging and developing personalities of children. How do such inevitable dislocations affect the personal stability of the child? What are the consequences, if any, for the child's later personality—could they be conducive to continuing wars or could they result in the inability of individuals to tolerate and permit wars?

3. Exact knowledge of social explosions, such as riots, as they occur or immediately after their occurrence. It would be important to know the personality structure of individuals involved in such social chaos. Is there a significant peculiarity of their personalities that is related to the personalities of individuals not involved? Are there any significant differences between an individual who participates in a

lynch mob or a race riot and one who does not or cannot? There is very little information on this significant social problem.

The hope for a dynamically stable, progressive, and constructive society lies in the ability of the social scientist to attack these and related problems with a vigor, a tough-mindedness, and a scrupulous regard for scientific integrity and freedom. It is the bias of science that answers to such important questions can be discovered by scientific methods. There is little doubt that social science has the ability to maintain a strict scientific direction. There is no doubt that scientific techniques and methods to study social phenomena are available and usable. The only doubt is whether swiftly moving social changes will permit the use of independent science or whether power and privilege will dominate, destroying man's freedom to think and to search for truth.

4

TOWARD A
UNIFYING
THEORY OF POWER

In 1938, in his book *Power, A New Social Analysis*, Bertrand Russell asserted that "the fundamental concept in social science is Power, in the same sense in which Energy is a fundamental concept in physics."

The laws of social dynamics, he said, can be understood only in terms of power and it was the obligation of a relevant social science to seek to discover these laws. It was necessary, also, to classify the forms of power and to study the ways in which individuals and organizations acquire control over men's lives. He defined power as "the production of intended effects" and distinguished among three forms of power: influence, the use of incentives and deterrents, and coercion.

One might have expected Russell's theory of this major problem in social science to have stimulated thought and research in social psychology in the three decades since its publication, for Bertrand Russell is one of the few extraordinary minds of this generation, indeed of western civilization.

But few social psychologists seem to be influenced by the reflections of philosophers, and a cursory review of the recent literature of social psychology reveals that power has been dealt with minimally as a theoretical problem and virtually not at all as an empirical one. There are a few exceptions. Herbert C. Kelman's discussion of communication and opinion change suggests that "pressure," interpreted as a type of power, is a significant intervening variable affecting the impact of the ideas of one person upon another.[1] John R. P. French equates power with force and influence: "The power of A over B is equal to maximum force which A can induce on B minus the maximum resisting force which B can mobilize in the opposite direction."[2] He develops theorems concerning the power of groups, the nature of communication patterns, and the role of leadership, but the problems themselves do not seem to be clarified by this seemingly premature resort to mathematical models. Dorwin Cartwright once stated that "the proposal that social technology may be employed to solve the problems of society suggests that social science may be applied in ways not different from those used in the physical sciences."[3] But this speculation, which is consistent with Bertrand Russell's earlier statement, has not been followed by research into social power as energy or indeed by further reflection in depth.

Cartwright paid justifiable tribute to the leadership of Kurt Lewin in seeking to make social psychology relevant to

1. Herbert C. Kelman, "Processes of Opinion Change," *Public Opinion Quarterly* 25 (1961): 57–78.

2. John R. P. French, "A Formal Theory of Social Power," *Psychological Review* 63 (1956): 181–194.

3. Dorwin Cartwright, "Achieving Change in People: Some Applications of Group Dynamics Theory," *Human Relations* 4 (1951): 381–396.

the pressing problems of the contemporary world. Lewin was indeed convinced of society's urgent need for a scientific approach to the understanding and the democratic control of the dynamics of social interaction. Unfortunately it does not seem to this observer that the field of social psychology has changed significantly since Lewin's death. Most social psychology is still primarily concerned with the investigation of isolated, trivial, and convenient problems rather than with those problems directly related to urgent social realities. Attitude and opinion research, sometimes disguised as communication analysis, still dominates the literature of social psychology. But opinion research, while concerned with some of the ingredients of power, takes no stand upon them, nor does it concern itself with the consequences of opinion in action. It may ask how many persons are willing to live next door to a Negro and how many have no opinion. It does not usually investigate what such persons actually do in a given situation nor does it explore the means of social change that would alter or sustain the direction of their behavior. This research dabbles in reality but avoids the real arena of action, and reflects, among other things, both a methodological sterility and a theoretical stagnation. Such preoccupation with methodological precision and measurement, reinforced by the inanimate energy of computers, appears to limit theoretical imagination and scientific creativity, and, therefore, social relevance.

Why have the bulk of social psychologists so far avoided or seemed to be reluctant to involve themselves in either a theoretical or empirical study of the problem of power?

The understandable human need for security may provide one answer, the dread of venturing into the unknown where dangers lurk, the personal fear of entering into controversy and conflict. The need of a relatively new discipline for security may be another factor. Just as one finds the retreat into jargon a characteristic of new disciplines like psychology and sociology which are struggling to achieve scientific status, particularly at a time when science is dominant as an instrument of power itself (in war, in peace, in government, in universities), so one finds a retreat into the preoccupation with language and with measurement in academic fields not sure of their place in the academic hierarchy. Psychology, sociology, political science—relatively new disciplines—are often afflicted with timidity and withdrawal symptoms, while even some of the oldest intellectual disciplines whose power has been slipping, e.g., philosophy, suffer similar anxiety patterns and adopt similar compensatory methods of response. Unfortunately, as insights from psychotherapy suggest, such solutions are no solutions at all, but simply reinforce the symptoms and convince the real world of the unreality and irrelevance of those who seek to escape its demands.

Other factors doubtless interfere with a re-evaluation of the basis of social psychology. To accept power as an important concept for research—or even as the unifying concept—would force social psychologists to rethink the rationale behind much present research. Social scientists, like other members of society, are not immune to social and intellectual inertia and resistance to change.

It may be argued that since power is an abstract, diffuse, and ambiguous phenomenon, it does not lend itself to objective empirical study or even to precise definition. If one defines the relevance and significance of a scientific problem in terms of the manifest and concrete aspects of a phenomenon and the currently available methodology, such an argument does seem persuasive. Yet, such an approach would have made impossible the development of scientific precision in the understanding and use of atomic physics. The concept of the atom as first postulated by Democritus was not based upon directly observable and manifest and concrete aspects of matter. Such fundamental concepts of physics as energy, electricity, and magnetism, such theories as relativity or the second law of thermodynamics, are primarily and essentially inferences. Even the reality itself, being nonempirical in its nature, must be judged often by consequences, not by the direct observation of a concrete substance. To demand that important aspects of reality meet the test of total concreteness—be directly perceivable and easily definable—is to exclude many if not the most important areas of reality from the province of scientific investigation.

Nor is it defensible to reject a scientific study of power because appropriate and precise methods of dealing with it do not now exist. One of the functions of science is to develop methods which *are* appropriate to the study of phenomena that seem worthy of investigation. A goal must be set before the means to reach it can be tested; goals are not to be rejected because the means is elusive. To limit the scope of scientific inquiry to such methods as already exist leads only to scientific stagnation. Even if one grants the limitations and inadequacy of present methodology, however, this would not explain the dearth of theoretical concern with social power in the field of social psychology.

The problem of power is fundamental and pervasive in man's interaction with his environment, within himself, in his interpersonal relations, in intergroup and international relations. Power permeates every aspect of human life; it is unavoidable. Perhaps its very pervasiveness leads to the attempt to avoid it—even to repress it psychologically—as a problem deserving serious and systematic theoretical analysis and empirical study. The psychologist may well feel threatened by a problem in which he participates as both subject and object. The student of social power must inevitably be a part of some power system himself; he cannot escape some degree of ego involvement. Problems of social power are necessarily related to problems of status, hierarchy, and privilege, and no human being can be outside a status hierarchy or a differential privilege system. To pretend otherwise must be seen as an empty, pathetic, escapist, and protective gesture.

A serious study of the problems of power might further require the social psychologist to become involved as an observer in social systems of which he himself is a part and of the status hierarchy within which he holds a status position, rather than merely to study some system "out there" or some primitive or exotic culture. But both anthropologists and psychologists usually believe that the acceptance of the value of detached objectivity requires that they explore only those systems with which they are not personally involved. How many American anthropologists have studied the ways of life in American rural areas or urban ghettos? Few other than Oscar Lewis or the specialists in the American Indian, and even in these cases the anthropologists are not directly involved with the group they themselves are studying. One could speculate whether the conclusion of moral relativity at which many cultural anthropologists arrive and which seems to influence other social scientists is not directly related to this lack of personal involvement. It would probably be quite difficult to maintain such a posture of cultural and moral relativity in dealing with the realities of a culture in which one has, oneself, been socialized and upon which one depends for his own personal security. This suggests a possible interpretation of the relativistic moral position as one not of objectivity but of indifference. Serious and relevant research on the problems of race relations, segregation, and desegregation, for example, would require social scientists to study not only racial attitudes and their determinants but also the more challenging and difficult problems of how a system of institutionalized prejudices is maintained and how it can be modified or destroyed. Indifference as to the result would be psychologically impossible.

The worship of a constricted concept of scientific objectivity; the need to protect oneself from the possibilities of status loss or the retaliatory use of power by those who are perceived as having, or presumed to have, greater power in our society; and the need to avoid involvement in power conflicts may all contribute significantly to the reluctance of social psychologists to tackle the problem of power as a legitimate area of scientific inquiry. One cannot study the problems of social power meaningfully with "total detachment." Conversely, if depersonalization and detachment are insisted upon as inviolable conditions for scientific objectivity and precision, then the problem of power cannot be studied scientifically.

The combination of these forces probably accounts for our failure to train graduate students in social psychology in ways of understanding and dealing with relevant and urgent social problems, such as poverty, desegregation, urban blight, political corruption, and international tensions. The attempt to disguise this desperate void in graduate training by making virtues of academic pedantry, qualified trivia, and sterile objectivity and by insisting that these are the hallmarks of pure research is recognized as ludicrous by reasonable men who have not themselves been educated to share the delusion. This delusion perpetuates itself but is no less a delusion because we who teach share it with or impose it upon our students.

Toward a Definition of Power

One of the first steps in the development of a systematic and scientific understanding of an observed phenomenon is an attempt to define the phenomenon in terms both clarifying and testable. The challenge to do this in relation to power is both formidable and unavoidable. Power permeates all human action and is elusive and not easily understood. All first definitions suffer necessarily from arbitrariness, tentativeness, and expendability. One can indeed interpret the task of *empirical science* as a continuous modification, that is, clarification or verification of theoretical definitions, and *theoretical science* as a continuous challenge to empirical research to prove it wrong.

There is no lack of attempts at a definition of social power, though those in the literature tend to come more often from sociologists, social philosophers, and political scientists than from social psychologists. The plethora and variety of definitions have contributed to the sense of the amorphousness or ambiguity of the concept. For example, Herbert Rosinski defines power as "nothing less than an objective quality of all reality, a quality inherent in all that exists by virtue of the mere fact that it does exist. Power is an inescapable

[73]

aspect of reality itself."[4] Beyond the fact that such a definition could apply to many other phenomena, even in the language of some theologians to a definition of God himself, the
definition is so comprehensive and inclusive as to make it
valueless for systematic research. Talcott Parsons tends to
emphasize social contract and sanctions in his definition of
power:

> Power then is generalized capacity to secure the perfor-
> mance of binding obligations by units in a system of
> collective organization when the obligations are legiti-
> mized with reference to their bearing on collective goals
> and where in case of recalcitrance there is a presumption
> of enforcement by negative situational sanctions—what-
> ever the actual agency of that enforcement.

For a group of other sociologists "decision making" char-
acterizes power. For C. Wright Mills power is inherent in
the ability to be "in command of the major hierarchies and
organizations of modern society," the ability "to make decisions which have major consequences." The difference
among Mills and Bierstedt and McIntosh, Lasswell and
Kaplan, seems one of degree and not of kind of decision
making.

Even a cursory view tends to the judgment that most
definitions of power are either tautological or so inclusive or
constrictive as to make difficult the development of subsidi-
ary hypotheses as a basis for systematic research, though
such limitations are undoubtedly a characteristic of all first
attempts. Perhaps it would be foolhardy then to attempt still
another definition of social power. Nonetheless, in the spirit

4. Herbert Rosinski, *Power and Human Destiny* (New York: Praeger,
1965).

which allegedly motivates mountain climbers to climb mountains, I hazard such an attempt in the hope that a theoretical approach might serve as a basis for systematic research and for its own modification and refinement, and lead, further, to the development of a relevant science of social psychology and an effective social technology.

It might be helpful to consider the definition of power found in physics as a point of departure. Power is defined in physics as any form of energy or force available for work or applied to produce motion or pressure. The concept of social power can be seen as essentially the same, namely the force or energy required to bring about, to sustain, or to prevent social, political, or economic change. Demonstration of the ability to achieve the desired change would be inherent in the definition of power. In its most fundamental sense, social power must be perceivable; it must be demonstrable. Pseudo power, verbal power, or substitute claims of power or denials of power would, therefore, be differentiated from power itself.

To the extent that this definition leans heavily on the demand for demonstration of the power to regulate social change and maintain social control, it is close to Max Weber's concept of power as the ability to control the behavior of others and an approach strongly influenced by the pragmatic behavioristic traditions in American psychology. It emphasizes not the ability to decide or the position of leadership—actually a *potential* source of power rather than *actual* power—but the uses and *consequences* on actual perceived social change.

A comprehensive theory of social power to be useful as a basis for social research must limit the practical area of concern—not because the theory is not large enough to encompass all uses of power, but because methods of research are more difficult to apply in some areas, as in war and revolution, which are special forms of intensive, coercive exercise of power impossible to study under systematic and controlled conditions. Psychiatrists are able to study with some effectiveness the trauma of battle, and psychologists the results of military psychological tests, but social psychological research, if relevant, would be concerned with the power implications of war itself. Conceivably social psychologists could study alternative approaches to the resolution of power conflicts other than through military means. This would be analogous to William James's "moral equivalent to war" and could be stated as the "power equivalent" to war. Clearly the power structure in the process of waging a war cannot encourage research into such alternatives. At present, social psychologists are confined to the personal observations of psychologists who participate in the conflict itself or to the research following conflict in the use of authority by occupation forces. So, too, social research on the nature and behavior of revolutions is limited. Project Camelot, which proposed to study the causes of revolution or other social change, was frustrated after American diplomats protested that such explosively controversial research appeared to other, sensitive nations as a new form of intellectual imperialism and invasion. The direct research problems are somewhat similar for social psychologists who seek a systematic understanding of domestic riots and other uncontrolled social disturbances.

Social power is defined here as that energy necessary to create, to sustain, or to prevent observable social change. Some tentative premises can be derived from this definition and they are presented as exploratory attempts at the development of a social psychological theory of power.

1. Power is *amoral;* it can be used, as can physical energy and nuclear power, for good or bad ends, but in itself it cannot determine value. It may be rational or irrational, *constructive* or *destructive,* in its consequences.

2. Power implies possibilities of choice in determining the priorities to be assigned to various individuals and groups within a social system of differential status and hierarchy in the gratification of needs, particularly of the status needs— under conditions not characterized by deprivation or stark scarcity of the means of satisfying more primary needs. It implies also the ability to make and implement such decisions and successfully to control resistance or attempts to impose counterdecisions.

3. Social power may manifest itself in varying degrees of intensity on a continuum from pseudo power of mere verbalization or claims of a power that does not in fact prevail in the face of conflict and cannot effect change in the desired direction; through latent power, which demonstrates itself only when challenged and to the minimal extent required to meet or contain the challenge; through active power, usually overt, understood, sustained, and institutionalized or generally mobilized in the face of continuing or anticipated challenges or conflicts; to coercive power, the enforcement of the desires of the holders of power in the face of overt, persistent, and intense challenges.

4. Power can be seen as operating in terms of a "law" of the economy of power. One observes that the power holders —the decision makers who determine the priorities and the

order and quality of need gratification in a given social system—do not expend any greater degree of power than that which is required to deal with the degree of challenge that confronts them. This hypothesis can be seen as an extension of the law of conservation of energy in physical systems and the principle of economy of effort in psychological and social systems. It would be violated only under the conditions of systemic personal instability, as in the case of the neurotic, the psychotic, or the brain-injured patient. Evidence of the violation of this principle in a social, or governmental, or international system would be found in any signs of the exercise of excessive power, that is, a power markedly disproportionate to the nature of the challenge, or employed under conditions in which there is no observable challenge or in which the excessive exercise of power itself generates the opposition. By its very violation it betrays the inherent instability, the tenuous integration, or the incipient disintegration of the system. Such an operational definition of authoritarianism or tyranny could provide the basis for an observable and verifiable concept of social pathology.

5. The conditions of passive or active resistance determine the degree of power exerted in any given situation. Power can be expressed in relatively innocuous ways, such as persuasion, argumentation, negotiation, and bargaining—largely verbal communication—where such methods work. It can be expressed in more direct ways in the actual control of the behavior of others, by institutional controls, restraints, sanctions, or privileges—under conditions in which verbal appeals and influence either do not work or cannot be risked. The confinement of powerless individuals to restrictive ghettos in the North can be seen as an example of power by control. Coercive power, farther along the continuum, tends

to be exerted only under the conditions of overt resistance to the less intense forms of power when a significant and sustained challenge arises to the status allocations, priority positions, and the implicit and explicit right of the power controllers to determine whether there will or will not be change. The law, the police, and other sanctioning institutions of the society operate with impunity in regulating the degree of dissent, challenge, or demand for change that is tolerable to those who control the power. The tactics used in the South to preserve the system of oppressive segregation were power by coercion. The further step beyond such coercive power would be sporadic or organized violence, and beyond this, or as a reaction to it, military power or revolution.

6. The forms, the manifestation, and the intensity of the social power exerted would vary according to the nature of the threat or according to the stability, the security, the psychological health and strength of the holders of power. Here, psychodynamics provides an adequate and stable model for the social psychologist concerned with a more systematic study of this problem. The problem of human motivation seems to me to be inextricable from if not identical with the problem of personal and social power. Adler's psychodynamic theory is an attempt to explain motivation and social interaction in terms of the striving for power, rooted in basic feelings of inferiority emerging inevitably from childhood impotence and dependence upon adults. Indeed, Adler's insistence upon the universality of various forms of compensation and "styles of life" which dominate the struggle for a tolerable sense of worth and dignity may be seen as the intra- and interpersonal level of social power. The implications of Adlerian theory for understanding per-

sonality development could provide the bridge for understanding and testing the relationship between a personal and familial level of power struggle and the social and intergroup level of power conflict and accommodation.

But such a leap poses a risk of psychological oversimplification of complex social problems. It is all too easy to assume that one understands social conflict through understanding the child's struggles to achieve a sense of worth in his conflict with punitive or overindulgent parents who equally constrict his ability to develop. Adult compensatory, self-protective, evasive, and escapist behavior may be so explained. But despite the evidence from such studies as Adorno's *The Authoritarian Personality*, and the immense amount of evidence and speculation from clinical experience, such explanations have not yet been verified. The promise of a unification of clinical and social psychology inherent in Adler's social dynamic theory and its influence on theorists and practitioners such as Karen Horney, Harry Stack Sullivan, and Erich Fromm can be fulfilled only with further research. So, too, must future research make more precise the relationship between Adler's insight of the struggle for power and the organismic motivational theory of Kurt Goldstein, who succeeded in incorporating the concepts of a neurophysiological psychology into a psychodynamic theoretical system of striving for self-fulfillment.

But even if the source of the motivation for power were understood, with its implications for redirecting such motivation, this still would not satisfy the need of social psychology to study the consequences of the uses of power. To understand the source is not to deal adequately with the resultant phenomenon—the various forms of power.

7. "Nonfunctional" forms of power, antipower, the de-

liberate non-use of power or nondecision, the hoarding of power, power waste and power atrophy, or power inertia, all may be effective techniques for determining or preventing change. Though it is difficult to determine the exact position on the continuum, some of these manifestations or nonmanifestations of power may be seen as affirmative attempts to influence the power equation. The refusal by political or religious leaders to use their power in a moral conflict or controversy is an empirically verifiable exercise in power and its consequences can be studied. These types of default of power could be called "The Deputy" Phenomenon. Power inertia, on the other hand, reflects the type of inhibition imposed upon the power controllers through the impingement of conflicting interests of equal intensity or appeal, a type of power blockage that seems similar to the phenomenon of abulia in abnormal psychology. Still another form of nonfunctional power is the dissipation of power through waste and atrophy. For example, while there have been both "strong" Presidents and "weak" Presidents in the American political system, the power inherent in the office has remained essentially the same, yet one could postulate that a prolonged waste of power implicit in an office could result in the erosion or the atrophy of the power of that office. These conditions may reflect weakness, instability, or decadence on the part of the sources and controllers of power.

8. Certain forms of power appear to be effective but in reality they are illusory pseudo power. Verbal posturing, unaccompanied by the ability to implement words in action, or the delusion of power, or the mistaken perception of power where it does not actually exist are pseudo power. In quiescent situations, pseudo power appears real, but in conflict or controversy the conscious or unconscious pretension

to power is seen to be ignored; it fails to prevail as a source of effective decision making, the implementation of decisions, or social change. Pseudo power ordinarily cannot sustain, or prevail, under conditions of prolonged protest or conflict. It is, in fact, the straw which may be given to and clutched by the powerless with impunity—and thereby tends to reduce to a minimum any realistic threat to the holders of actual power.

9. The voluntary transfer or sharing of power may also be illusory. This phenomenon poses many problems which relate to questions of motivation, the conditions under which voluntary sharing of power exists, and the extraordinarily difficult question of the extent to which there is, in fact, any sharing or transfer that is not a reflection of an underlying power conflict and an attempt at resolution involving the "law" or principle of the economy of power. An example would be the withdrawal of colonial control over previously dependent states. It is generally accepted that European nations have voluntarily yielded political control to these "emerging nations," but they nonetheless often retain economic power there. When power is "shared" by the dominant, it may be that what is shared is the appearance rather than the substance of power. If the other side of the equation, the nondominant, believes in the reality and seeks the substance of power, conflict tends to reappear or increase. The civil rights struggle in America may raise precisely this same dilemma for the present holders of power.

A UNIFYING THEORY OF POWER

In an integrated and efficient social system, significant clusters or reservoirs of power tend to operate as a dynamic

Gestalt, each contributing to the unity and power of the whole social system despite the possibility and the actuality of conflicts among them. The interaction of differentiated and at times competing forces is directed toward the end of maintaining an integrated system. Serious internal or external threats almost invariably result in the mobilization of these various aspects of power to protect and preserve the system. From one perspective, this process would seem inimical to change—the maintenance of an essentially static state. This would be social stagnation. However, under certain, at present unclear, conditions, a given power source or a combination of power sources can exercise individual or combined power to bring about significant and desired changes in the total system, not only without any serious risk of disintegration but with an increase in the integrity and stability of the social system. This would reflect a dynamic and constructive role of competing power clusters within the power Gestalt of the larger social system. This could be viewed as the basis of social viability and growth.

The significant clusters of power in American society are governmental; economic; religious; the perceived cohesive power of group identification, e.g., ethnic power; and voluntary organizational power, e.g., the American Medical Association. Beyond these, intellectual power manifests itself through the prestige and influence of educational institutions and through the "expertise" of technological scientists called upon by government and industry for consultation or "decision making" or of respectability. The power of the "critical," "nonco-opted" intellectual is presently unclear. That his role is related in some way to power is suggested by the persistent anti-intellectualism of our society, which selects the "critical" rather than the co-opted intellectual as the primary object of attack and neutralization. Power is manifest also in related phenomena. Propagandistic power studied extensively by social psychologists, no doubt in part because the prevalence and manageability of the evidence (newspapers, books, television, opinion polls, etc.) make research neater and more easily encompassed; the power of personality, leadership through prestige, authority, charisma —all of these must be taken into account in a theory of power. The peculiar combination that leads to significant social change without disintegration must be isolated and understood.

A theory of power could serve not only as a unifying principle for social psychology but as a unifying principle for social science as a whole. There is an immediate and urgent need for the development of such a unifying theoretical approach if the field of social psychology itself is not to be relegated to an irrelevant, if not ludicrous level of ad hoc investigations of the type of trivial problems which lend themselves to the collection and tabulation of data obtained from the captive audience of undergraduate students. A unifying theory of power might provide the basis for the theoretical and empirical integration of the fields of developmental, clinical, and social psychology.

Although social psychologists in general have shrunk from considering the nature and consequences of social power, other social scientists have been less reticent. In sociology, studies of community leadership and power structure studies, analyses of the behavior of small groups, investigations of military leadership, and the like have shown—in the work of the Lynds, Talcott Parsons, Robert Merton, C. Wright Mills, George Caspar Homans, and others—real concern for problems of social power. In political science the

[84]

nature of leadership is under growing scrutiny, in theory and in empirical studies, as in the work of Richard Neustadt, James MacGregor Burns, Louis Koenig, Clinton Rossiter, among others, which have shown genuine fascination with the ways of power. In economics, scholars like Peter Drucker, John K. Galbraith, and Adolf Berle have reflected on power as a force in economic matters and in society as a whole.

The need is for greater unity of theory and research among the disciplines in the social sciences. Problems like those of power cannot be understood from only one perspective and only one set of facts—the skills and wisdom of all the disciplines must be joined if social science is to develop a theoretical and functional understanding of social power.

In a theory of power as a basis of social science research the distinction between pure and applied research with all of its status implications must disappear. Such a separation is artificial and meaningless. Not only must the disciplines themselves be unified in such a theory of power, but the fragmentation within research itself must be dissolved.

The phenomenon of power can provide a basis for meaningful rather than *pro forma* interdisciplinary theoretical communication and research, obliterating those arbitrary lines of rigid differentiation among social scientists which are sustained by petty status distinctions, by trivial power concerns, and by sheer lack of imagination and the inability to grasp the coherence of ideas.

Yet there is danger. One political scientist preparing to write a biography of Kennedy before his nomination and election was warned by some of his colleagues that it was impossible to write objectively about a subject with which one was subjectively involved; they argued even that such biographies should never be written about the living, that political science owed no such responsibility to the electorate. The controversy aroused by the publication of Arthur Schlesinger, Jr.'s book *A Thousand Days,* a detailed and intimate analysis of the decision-making process during the Kennedy administration, reflects similar problems. Indeed, the risks are great. When one is involved and cares about the consequences, it is harder to be objective. All the more reason not to avoid the challenge.

Individual social sciences which maintain the posture of scientific purity through studied detachment from the problems of society may maintain and reinforce this posture by the luxury of isolation from other social sciences. The cult of specialization within disciplines can be seen as an extension of this concept of the nature of scientific purity which brings with it the increased status gains of isolation and social irrelevance. Applied social science cannot afford these luxuries of isolation or detachment or any definition of scientific objectivity or precision based upon them. Socially relevant social sciences must run the risks of loss of status—if scientific status is to be determined by preoccupation with irrelevant and trivial problems—by seeking to define and solve such basic survival problems of our society as power, empathy, justice, and other determinants of social viability or stagnation, creativity or destruction. It is from this perspective that the nature, methods, and problems of interdisciplinary work among social scientists emerge as serious but by no means insoluble problems.

One can start from the assumption that man's fellow man can be as much of a threat to human survival as the impersonal forces of his biological and physical environment. It would be incumbent upon man, therefore, in attempting to understand and control his social environment, to use the same or similar methods as those employed in dealing with the physical environment: supernaturalism, magic, animism, religion, philosophy, and eventually science and technology. These have in common the fact that they are attempts on the part of man to use his intelligence as the chief instrument for the understanding, resolving, and controlling of those forces in his environment which threaten his survival.

The social environment, like the physical and biological environment, is a Gestalt of interrelated forces. The complexity of this Gestalt defies the limits of human observation and intelligence. If man is to maintain the arrogance of intellectual and technological control over his environment, he must use his intelligence to break down the complexity of reality into understandable and manageable components. Hence the emergence of disciplines—reflecting not the nature of reality but the limitation of human observation, intelligence, and probably time and energy; the compartmentalized and separate discipline approach to human understanding has contributed to progress in understanding the nature of the whole, the complexity of the Gestalt of reality, and has led to the demonstrable ability of man to control many of the threatening forces of his physical, biological, and social environments.

But, when confronted with major, prolonged, or epidemic crises, man must pool the knowledge from the separate disciplines and seek to control these threatening forces if he is to survive. Contemporary man appears to be threatened by a variety of social forces which must now be approached by a multiplicity of disciplines. The artificial distinctions among the social sciences are no more adaptive now than were artificial distinctions among the biological sciences when the main threats to man were plagues and epidemics. The model of the pooling of physical science and mathematical knowledge which ushered in the nuclear age—and paradoxically increased survival threats due to social and moral ignorance —must now become the basis for an effective interdisciplinary approach to the solution of social problems. Social sciences can no longer afford the precious isolation or the pretenses of the quest for mathematical precision. The clear and immediate dangers to the survival of human civilization demand interdisciplinary coordination of the work of social scientists. The problems are the same—the conditions essential for human survival. The importance of division of labor in seeking solutions to these problems cannot be argued. The systematic pooling of information as a basis for further experiments, policy, and action is now mandatory.

The fact that a functional approach to interdisciplinary work is now mandatory does not mean that it will be achieved without severe difficulties. The traditional perspective which led to the intellectually convenient fractionation of reality is a major barrier. But this barrier must be breached and is likely to be breached by the persistence and intensification of the problems which can be solved only through the systematic and disciplined use of human intelligence.

The rigid organization of colleges and universities along departmental lines resists genuine and interdisciplinary research and action. The tendency of academics, including academic social scientists, to define scholarship and scientific precision in terms of safety and isolation from the dangers of the political and economic arenas—in terms of blissful and precious intellectual and moral estrangement from the problems of the real world—results in the production of students unprepared to contribute directly to social solutions. These students must be trained—and at times untrained and retrained after they leave the universities—if they are to work effectively in an interdisciplinary setting. Artificial departmental barriers, rivalries, lack of communication exist as the norm, with some exceptions, within the walls of academia. For such reasons, institutions which seek to foster genuine applied interdisciplinary research, directing themselves to the solutions of social problems and therefore to social policy, social action, and social change, should probably at present be set up outside of university settings or should insist upon maximum autonomy from university administrative controls and institutional arrangements.

There are many areas where social psychologists might direct their energies profitably toward a study of power: a study of power conflict and resistance; the nature of victory and defeat, of acquiescence and accommodation; institutionalization and the regulation of conflict; intensification of conflicts; and the pseudo resolution of conflicts through deflection, through escape valves and through regulated emotional catharsis. Social psychologists might ask even more fundamental questions such as: What do we mean by social change? What are stable criteria by which the idea of progress can be demonstrated as a fact in human social interaction? To what extent is perceived change or verbalization of change a reflection of the reality of change? Does significant social change occur under conditions without conflict? What are the fundamental value problems which underlie these questions?

Such questions are raised on the basis of a faith by no means yet verified that a scientific understanding of the dynamics of society can lead toward a rational control of society consistent with democracy and with respect for the dignity and uniqueness of humanity.

The choice for society as a whole, as well as for social science, is between capricious lawlessness, pre-scientific in its random patterns of change, and rational law, scientific in its plan for controlling the reality, rate, and direction of change. Social science has a stake in such rational planning, for without research into the consequences of alternative actions and without imaginative theories derived from or stimulating such research, society cannot predict what its choices will achieve and cannot make reasonable decisions as to the best strategy for the fulfillment of human needs. Once social science and society as a whole have opted for rational planning—and resisted the anti-intellectualism of drift and impulse—they must decide between authoritarian planning, like the planning in Walden Two, in which the capacity for reason itself is denied to all but a few, and democratic planning, in which men are not conditioned like rats to be happy according to master plan, but are encouraged to achieve the fullest measure of their own ability to think, to be troubled, to grow, and to develop their capacity to respond with depth of feeling and understanding. But to meet the challenge of the constant danger of authoritarian control—even that which wears the cloak of benevolence—by regressing to the earlier level of capricious irrationality is for social science to betray society and its own purposes out of lack of faith in human potential. Rational control is inevitable and the real test is which philosophy will guide its direction. At present, many of the most democratically minded social psychologists—as may be said to be true of political liberals—find conflict and controversy distasteful and rational control antithetical to their democratic faith.

Because they do, they frequently leave the field to those less tender of mind, for whom Brave New Worlds and 1984 are interesting exercises in power, not to be condemned out of hand. They may leave the field of psychology to those who think man a creature of animal reflex, without mind or soul, to be manipulated for his own good through reward and punishment. Social psychologists cannot leave such important decisions to those who see psychology only as a strategy for mechanistic control and mindless reinforcements.

Rational planning is not to be confused with mechanistic control of man and society. The use of the approach and methods of a truly relevant social science for the development of a democratic social technology can increase human effectiveness and is probably essential to social survival; and it can be consistent with human dignity. Mechanistic manipulation of man, on the other hand, unquestionably dehumanizes.

The ultimate question, asked by Plato centuries ago, is: Can the rational and intellectual powers of man provide the power to control the irrational primitive and destructive forces? Upon the answer to this question rests the destiny of human civilization.

5

—✦—

SOCIAL RESEARCH AND
SOCIAL POLICY:
THE *BROWN* DECISION AND
ITS AFTERMATH, A CASE STUDY

A SIGNIFICANT CASE STUDY in the use of social science for the achievement of social change occurred in the legal strategy that led to the *Brown* decision. The case reflected all of the potential for change and the attendant risks that a theory of social power would anticipate.

The inevitable sober reflection that followed the enthusiasm of a momentous victory revealed some challenging theoretical, methodological, and research problems which had to be faced and solved by contemporary social psychologists if they were to fulfill the promise of significant social contributions.

In a very real sense, social scientists and social psychologists unexpectedly found themselves in a role not unlike that of the physicists. Surely our position was not quite as dramatic—nor were our activities yet as circumscribed and controlled by political considerations, probably because the effects of our contributions on shifts in the balance and

[92]

structure of social power had not yet been fully recognized by political and industrial leaders.

The role of social science in the *Brown* decision was crucial, in the Supreme Court's opinion, in supplying persuasive evidence that segregation itself means inequality. Social psychologists had testified in the courts as expert witnesses (most extensively in the Virginia case) on the effects of segregation on personality development, on the effects of school segregation in lowering motivation to learn, on the consequences of desegregation, and on other questions. I examined the Negro children involved in several of the cases to determine whether evidence of personality distortion related to racial discrimination and segregation could be ascertained. At the request of the NAACP, psychologists also prepared an appendix to the NAACP appellants' brief ("The Effects of Segregation and the Consequences of Desegregation: A Social Science Statement") endorsed by thirty-two social scientists, psychologists, and psychiatrists (my role was to serve as liaison between the lawyers and the social psychologists). The introduction of social science testimony in these cases proved to be a significant extension of legal frontiers.

The essential questions faced by the Supreme Court were not questions of legal precedent, historical in nature, but questions relating to the social consequences of legally imposed segregation. Without such evidence, the Court could only speculate about the probable damage caused by the violation of constitutional rights implicit in segregated education. The social scientists testified to the damage inherent in the total pattern of segregation on the human personality. On the basis of their testimony, the Court held that separate educational facilities are inherently unequal because they are separate. By providing such evidence, the social scientists made it possible to avoid the need to obtain proof of individual damage and to avoid assessment of the equality of facilities in each individual school situation. The assumption of inequality could now be made wherever segregation existed.

In this regard it must now be stated that in doing so the Court, which appeared, in the 1954 decision, to rely on the findings of social scientists, rejected these findings in handing down the 1955 implementation decision. An empirical study of various forms and techniques of desegregation suggested that the gradual approach to desegregation did not increase its chances of success or effectiveness. The findings further suggested that forthright, direct desegregation within the minimum time required for the necessary administrative changes tended to facilitate the process. Gradualism or any form of ambiguity and equivocation on the part of those with the power of decision is interpreted by the segregationists as indecision and provides them with the basis for increasing resistance, as well as giving them time to organize, intensify, and prolong their opposition. In this regard, it is relevant to note that the pattern of massive resistance and sporadic, violent opposition to desegregation occurred after the 1955 decision. There is no evidence that a more direct, specific, and concrete implementation decree would have resulted in any more tension, procrastination, or evasion than the seemingly rational, statesmanlike "deliberate speed" decision of the Court. It does not seem likely that the pace of public school desegregation could have been slower.

The United States Supreme Court, however, having once accepted social science data, not only opened the door to further use of such data but placed a heavy burden of responsibility upon individual social scientists and their professional associations.

The closer and more direct relationship between social science and social action, policy, and change demanded a re-examination of some of our previous assumptions and premises. Chief among the issues which had to be re-evaluated were: (1) arguments between the protagonists of pure versus applied science, (2) the nature of scientific objectivity, and (3) the role of moral values in social science.

The distinction between pure versus applied research had become less and less clear in the social sciences as it had in the physical and biological sciences. This at best artificial distinction could not stand up against the only valid test of science—a quest for understanding and verification. The trite arguments of purists were revealed as serving the function of bolstering sagging scientific egos in an attempt to save them from the intolerable recognition of a sense of irrelevance or futility. Truth is always useful—either immediately or eventually.

Some of the theoretical, methodological, and research considerations highlighted by the involvement of social psychologists in the *Brown* decision were these:

1. A critical re-examination of the mores, folkways, attitudes approach to the understanding of social behavior and as factors in the prediction of social change. Do these concepts contribute to our understanding of behavioral changes? Are they necessary antecedents to social change? What are the conditions under which verbal attitudes and opinions do or do not influence behavior?

2. What are the specific roles of leaders, authority figures,

propaganda, and education in blocking or facilitating changes in personal behavior and social changes?

3. How can one interpret the studies which present evidence showing that attitudinal changes accompany changes in social situations?

4. What contributions to an understanding of social behavior and accommodation to changes in society can come from learning theory? What contributions can empirical study of social changes make to learning theory?

5. In what way and how do adverse social situations influence personality? Precise answers to this question would demand more systematic studies of personality modifications under conditions of acute and chronic social stress and would increase our knowledge of the basis for differences in reactions to pathological social situations, e.g., racial segregation, economic deprivation, and other forms of social injustices and catastrophic social situations.

Related questions are: How do human beings adjust and accommodate to significantly changed social situations? What are the direction and intensity of initial reaction? What is its duration? What are the signs and determinants of eventual accommodation? Answers to these questions would throw light on the problems of the nature of human inertia and on resistance to change as well as on the phenomena of human modifiability or the capacity for or susceptibility to change.

We could no longer avoid realistic, systematic, and tough-minded studies of such basic psychological and social problems as the nature, distribution, and salience of the ethical and empathic sense in man. How do these influence or fail to influence the behavior of individuals and groups?

Social action and social research can no longer be discrete and incompatible. The role of the social sciences demonstrates the validity of Kurt Lewin's insistence upon action-research as an indispensable tool of verification in the social sciences. Society is the laboratory of the social psychologist. Social processes are the phenomena he cannot avoid studying. Studying fragments—usually safe ones—of society or of individuals leads to conceptual and interpretative errors and, therefore, to inaccurate predictions.

Out of the demands upon the social psychologists to test their theories and research findings in the cold, critical, and demanding light of practical social issues came the need for continuing re-examination and re-evaluation of theoretical assumptions and premises, the development of newer and more effective empirical methods, and more precise knowledge and more accurate predictions.

We can do this only by continued dedication to an unfettered search for truth. A search that must remain free—directly or indirectly, flagrantly or insidiously—from big governments and political expediency, from big foundations and their effective restrictions of scientific inquiry through their power to encourage or discourage certain research by control of funds, from big business concern with immediately practical, useful, or eventually profitable research findings, and from social action and reform agencies, which are friendly to science under certain circumstances but may not be so friendly when circumstances change.

Social psychologists must be free of these subtle or overt potential constrictions and impediments. Like other social scientists we must be increasingly clear in our standards of scientific integrity and our standards of social morality.

We could not afford to be seduced by the flattering pro-

[97]

testations of those who came to pay us court after *Brown,* bringing gifts of grants, subsidies, and praise.

It was clear in the mid-1950s that professional organizations should set up machinery to prevent abuses and prostitution of "science" in subsidized research, litigation, and social policy decisions, and that such machinery should be geared to prevent our becoming more shackled or aligned to the power competition, to political expediency; we must not become a mere tool of the power structure. The procedures and ethics of social science involvement in social problems needed to be spelled out clearly, and in such a way as to guard against flagrant abuses without at the same time constricting necessary scientific independence, integrity, and the free exercise of personal judgment and conscience.

After footnote eleven of the *Brown* decision acknowledged the contribution of social science to the Court's findings, a significant debate ensued in legal and social science circles on the appropriateness of reliance on such testimony and on the accuracy of the evidence itself.

Interestingly enough, such controversy had not arisen earlier about the role of social science in industry, in government, or in the military. The fact that social science was now participating in social change in ways that raised questions about the fundamental injustice of American society and the power arrangements that supported it was probably not irrelevant to the anxiety such participation now aroused.

One of the most serious and consistent criticisms came from distinguished professor of jurisprudence Edmond Cahn of New York University Law School.[5] Cahn questioned the contribution of the social scientists' testimony to the decision

5. See chapter on Jurisprudence, Annual Survey of American Law, *New York University Law Review* 30 (1955): 150.

and implied that their primary motive was not "strict fidelity to objective truth." The fact, however, was that the social scientists were careful to reject findings that could not be substantiated. Professor Cahn seemed to suggest that legal facts and scientific facts were two kinds of reality. This we could not accept. For us there was but one order of reality, and science and law were parts of it.

The most serious criticism, however, began to come from social scientists. Dr. Bruno Bettelheim of the University of Chicago stated publicly that there is no scientific evidence that racial segregation damages the human personality.[6] In view of the effect of Nazi concentration camps on their inmates—a primary subject of Dr. Bettelheim's own research—it is hard to understand the rationale for this statement. But it was Dr. Ernest van den Haag of the New School for Social Research who presented the most intense and specific criticism from social scientists questioning the validity of the evidence.[7] He assumed that science could not assess personality damage associated with social stigma, a curious position for a contemporary social scientist to hold.

On the whole, none of the criticism has offered solid evidence to refute the psychologists' appendix to the legal brief in *Brown*. The testimony offered then still stands.

Those who attempt to use the methods of social science in dealing with problems which threaten the status quo must expect opposition and even retaliation. They must be prepared to accept the risks their role entails. But to assume that such involvement is by definition unscientific is to

6. "Discrimination and Science," review of *Prejudice and Your Child*, *Commentary* 21 (April 1956): 384.

7. Ernest van den Haag and Ralph Ross, *The Fabric of Society* (New York: Harcourt, Brace & World, 1957), Appendix to chapter 14, "Prejudice about Prejudice."

betray the ideal goal of science itself, which is a total concern for truth wherever it may lead, whatever it may threaten. The valid goals of law and science are identical—to secure for man personal fulfillment in a just, stable, and viable society.

THE SOCIAL SCIENCE AFTERMATH OF THE *Brown* DECISION

Yet the potential for change inherent in the *Brown* decision has been only partially fulfilled, ironically more in the South than in the North. The belief that the *Brown* decision would be enforced in good faith, in ways consistent with sound administrative and educational practices, and with due regard to constitutional safeguards and the respect for law essential to a stable democratic government, has not been supported by the evidence and events of the intervening years. Rather, public school desegregation has been aborted, evaded, subjected to the mockery of tokenism, equivocation, and seemingly endless litigation, while generations of Negro children in these segregated schools continue to be damaged irrevocably.

The nation, generally, and those social scientists who fought for the *Brown* decision have tended to underplay the extent to which racism has been internalized in American society, not only institutionally but also in the degree of intensity that contaminates almost all human beings socialized in America. Initially, the attempt was to use the *Brown* decision as a form of therapy, to free American whites and Negroes from the depths of the disease. It became apparent, however, that the extent of the metastasis had been underestimated and misunderstood, that the pattern of resistance, evasion, and tokenism that followed *Brown* could be explained only by a racism that had rotted the roots of American life North and South. Acknowledgment of the intensity and extent of the disease may, however, be positive in its effects. The North has, at the least, become more honest in its racism; it no longer hides behind the posture of non-racism. That may be an important first step toward genuine social change.

The effort of the challenging NAACP brief in *Brown* to point also to the destructive influences of racism upon the dominant white culture was virtually ignored by the Court as well as by social scientists and the public.

With reference to the impact of segregation and its concomitants on children of the majority group, the report indicates that the effects are somewhat more obscure. Those children who learn the prejudices of our society are also being taught to gain personal status in an unrealistic and non-adaptive way. When comparing themselves to members of the minority group, they are not required to evaluate themselves in terms of the more basic standards of actual personal ability and achievement. The culture permits and, at times, encourages them to direct their feelings of hostility and aggression against whole groups of people the members of which are perceived as weaker than themselves. They often develop patterns of guilt feelings, rationalizations and other mechanisms which they must use in an attempt to protect themselves from recognizing the essential injustice of their unrealistic fears and hatreds of minority groups.

The report indicates further that confusion, conflict, moral cynicism, and disrespect for authority may arise in majority group children as a consequence of being taught the moral, religious and democratic principles of the brotherhood of man and the importance of justice and fair play by the same persons and institutions who, in their support of racial segregation and related practices, seem to be acting in a prejudiced and discriminatory manner. Some individuals may attempt to resolve this conflict by intensifying their hostility toward the minority group. Still others react by developing an unwholesome, rigid, and uncritical idealization of all authority figures—their parents, strong political and economic leaders. As described in *The Authoritarian Personality*, they despise the weak, while they obsequiously and unquestioningly conform to the demands of the strong whom they also, paradoxically, subconsciously hate.[8]

Racism at that time was acknowledged primarily in terms of its damage to the victims of oppression; the moral and psychological erosion of the oppressor himself had not been faced. The implications of the Myrdal report, *An American Dilemma*, published in 1944, had not yet been carried out in social science or the law.

Racism emerges in both blatant and in more difficult to answer, subtle manifestations. In the academic community, it began to be clear in the 1960s that apparently sophisticated and compassionate theories used to explain slow Negro student performance might themselves be tainted with racist condescension. Some of the theories of "cultural deprivation," "the disadvantaged," and the like, until re-

8. "The Effects of Segregation and the Consequences of Desegregation: A Social Science Statement," Appendix to Appellants' Briefs, Brown v. Board of Education, as quoted in Kenneth B. Clark, *Prejudice and Your Child*, revised edition (Boston: Beacon Press, 1955), p. 168.

cently popular in educational circles and in high governmental spheres, and still prevalent in fact, were backed for the most part by inconclusive and fragmentary research and much speculation. The eagerness with which such theories were greeted was itself a subtle racist symptom. The theories obscured this orientation, but when challenged, some of their advocates posed more overt racist formulations.

The earliest explanations of the academic inferiority of Negro children had been given in terms of their inherent, racially determined intellectual inferiority. This approach not only dominated the thinking of laymen but was accepted and reinforced by the theories of educators and social scientists until the fourth decade of the twentieth century. It was not until the publication of the significant research and interpretations of Boas and Klineberg in the 1930s that such subtle or flagrant theories of inherent racial inferiority ceased to be fashionable among social scientists.

With the increasing acceptance of the Boas and Klineberg findings, social and environmental explanations of the academic retardation of Negro children replaced racial and biological explanations in the literature of the social sciences, reflecting the general rise of liberal thought that characterized the decade.

The most recent specific explanation of the academic retardation of Negro children, the "cultural deprivation" theory, the contemporary form of environmental interpretations, rejects explanations of inherent racial or biological inferiority and asserts that the total pattern of racial prejudice, discrimination, and segregation found in a racist society blocks the capacity of school personnel to teach minority group children with the same observable efficiency as that given other children. These children may, therefore, be expected to remain academically retarded no matter how well they are taught. Among the specific barriers emphasized by different writers in varying degrees are: environmentally determined sensory deficiencies; withdrawn or hyperactive behavior; low attention span; peculiar or bizarre language patterns; lack of verbal stimulation; absence of father or stable male figure in the home; and lack of books in the home.

In spite of the fact that these factors have dominated the literature and have been frequently repeated and generally accepted as explanations of the academic retardation of lower-status children, they have not been verified as causal factors through any precise and systematic research reported in the published literature. The evidence, or indeed lack of evidence, suggests, therefore, that this concept has gained acceptance through intuition, general impressions, and repetition.

The provocative work of Pasamanick may be an exception to this general observation.[9] He and his colleagues have sought to define the general problem of cultural deprivation in terms of poverty, namely the effects of nutritional deficiencies in the inadequate diets of low-income pregnant females on the neurological development of prenatal and postnatal children. This approach, if verified by further more systematic and controlled research, will provide a very sophisticated combination of biological, physiological, neurological, and social environmental variables in the explanation of the academic retardation of low-income and low-status children.

9. Benjamin Pasamanick and Hilda Knobloch, "The Contribution of Some Organic Factors to School Retardation in Negro Children," *Journal of Negro Education* 27 (1958): 4.

Many students of this problem have asserted that motivation is the pivotal factor in the relationship between low socioeconomic status—"cultural deprivation"—and academic retardation. They maintain that low-status children are not motivated toward academic success and therefore do not perform up to the level of more privileged children. An analysis of the literature containing this motivation explanation of the problem leaves many important questions unanswered.

Is the low motivation of low-status children a primary factor directly reflecting their low socioeconomic or racial status? Is the low motivation of these children peculiar to them—and specific to low academic performance? Is low academic motivation a consequence of low academic performance which in turn is caused by other factors?

It is important to obtain these answers because imperative changes in educational policy and practices which will affect the lives of human beings will be determined by them. Cultural deprivation theorists have not only provided the public school educational establishment with a respectable rationalization for maintaining the status quo of educational inefficiency for low-status children, but the related technology of this theory—compensatory or educational enrichment programs—appears to provide the basis for inherent contradictions in its premises and assumptions.

An uncritical acceptance of this theory and explanation seems to be contradicted by:

1. The concretely demonstrated psychological fact of the normal curve in the distribution of human intellectual potential, personality characteristics, motivation, and other personal characteristics believed to be related to academic performance.

2. The modifiableness of human beings.

3. The fact that normal human beings who are taught, motivated to learn, expected to learn, and provided with conditions conducive to learning, will learn up to or near the limits of their capacity.

Furthermore, the cultural deprivation theories are clear violations of the law of parsimony, since they seek more complex explanations without determining that more simple explanations are not adequate. Cultural deprivation theories appear to bypass more direct and specific educational variables, such as quality of teaching and supervision, acceptance or rejection of the students by teachers, and educational methods and facilities.

Given the history of educational rejection of Negro children, it would seem obvious to one trained in the methods of science that such more direct variables would have to be held constant and checked out with more precision and more sensitive instruments than the widely quoted Coleman report[10] does before one could resort to the more elaborate, ambiguous, and seemingly uncontrollable catchall variable of cultural deprivation. In this regard it is significant that the literature, while eloquent and repetitive in its expansion of the cultural deprivation hypothesis, is almost totally silent on discussions or research which seek to determine the relationship between subtle or flagrant rejection of a child by his teachers because of race, color, economic status, and family income, and the level of his academic performance. These social, psychological, and educational variables seem worthy

10. James Coleman et al., *Equality of Educational Opportunity* (Washington, D.C.: Office of Education, United States Department of Health, Education, and Welfare, 1966).

of a serious attention and research which they have not as yet received. The cultural deprivation explanation did not emerge in its present form until the 1950s and did not receive wide currency and general uncritical acceptance until after the *Brown* decision. It has since become an integral part of the controversy concerning the quality of education provided for Negro children in de jure and de facto segregated schools.

Such theories are often regarded as liberal because they posit environmental inadequacy rather than genetic inferiority and because they are often used to support demands for integration. The problem, exemplified by the Coleman report, which takes this approach, is that it concludes that it is the environmentally caused characteristics of white children which are the positive component of integrated schools, and that Negro children gain educationally primarily from association with white children. Further research is necessary to determine whether correlation and causal factors have been confused in this important study, but perhaps most important, it is necessary to study the majority white school as a total unit as compared to the majority Negro school, to determine what happens in the school itself *because* white children are present. Sensitive instruments must be sought to measure teacher and administrative expectations, counseling attitudes, quality of curriculum, and the like; but beyond the assessment of these individual factors, it is necessary to evaluate the total pattern of advantage and of deprivation. On the basis of years of observation and research of ghetto education, I would advance the proposition that one would find a significantly high correlation between a pattern of deprivation and ghetto schools, and a pattern of advantage and white urban and suburban schools. It is not the white child per se whose presence leads to higher achievement for the Negro child who associates with him in class, but the quality of the education provided because the white child is there that makes the difference, or so I believe the empirical evidence indicates. To argue, without irrefutable proof, that this is not the case is to lend support to a racially defined environmental theory of academic achievement that is no less callous in its consequences than a genetic theory of racial inferiority would be.

In the fields of sociology, history, and anthropology racial insensitivity has taken other forms. One is the "bootstrap" argument ("We did it, why can't you?"), which assumes class more significant than race in determining status in America. Its proponents urge Negroes to climb the ladder of success in imitation of the experience of upward mobility of the other ethnic groups; the implication is that failure to succeed can be laid at the door of the group that fails. Another is the pluralistic argument, which assumes that voluntary separatism is the genius of American democracy, and that the Negro's demand for integration is a threat to the pluralistic tradition and aspirations of various ethnic groups.

The problem here is that both theories obscure or deliberately evade the fact that the Negro's inferior status, unlike that of other American citizens, was historically fixed by law and reinforced by the cult of racism. The Negro was highly visible as the white immigrant was not. The Negro, unlike the white immigrant, had to overcome centuries of slavery, the reinforcement of inferior status in the post-Reconstruction conspiracy led by powerful political, financial, and real estate interests, and the continuing pattern of institutionalized racial oppression in the twentieth century. The Negro could not become indistinguishable from other Americans merely by changing his name, his speech, his style. Color was his continuing badge of inferiority.

The Negro has not been permitted pluralistic interaction. He has been restricted from integrated or equal status. It is only recently that Negroes have been permitted to function in colleges and universities in even limited numbers. W. E. B. Du Bois, as great an intellect as America has produced, was never invited to teach at Harvard, his alma mater. Only recently have Negroes—in limited numbers—been admitted to high governmental positions. Negroes are still not admitted to the highest financial circles. Pluralism, if indeed it is desirable, must follow not precede integration, for it is meaningful only in a context of limited voluntary separation under conditions where all share in the necessarily integrated economic and educational system. Therefore, to argue for pluralism—when the status of the Negro is unequal—is to obscure injustice. Pluralism without equality would best be described by the caste model. The untouchables in stratified India lived in a pluralistic society of a kind. Calls for pluralism just at the time when the Negro is demanding full freedom of entrance into previously restricted neighborhoods, into previously insular colleges, into previously white-monopolized governmental employment, must be viewed with a suspicion that equal interaction is not the intent of white society.

The new theories of the genetic inferiority of Negroes, like those posed by Arthur Jensen,[11] are almost identical to the

11. "How Much Can We Boost I.Q. and Scholastic Achievement?" *Harvard Educational Review* 39 (Winter, 1969): 1–123.

old, their statistical apparatus notwithstanding. And like the old, they are not verifiable:

1. Because the concept of race itself is so elusive for certain distinct physical characteristics—which themselves vary widely within and between groups—that genetic differences identifiable by race have so far proved impossible to determine.

2. Because even if pure racist differences were ascertainable, the Negro is not a biological or "racial" entity. The American Negro is a historical intermixture—of white and Indian and African.

3. Because the American Negro as a socially defined group with common characteristics generated by social and institutional exclusiveness has existed for too brief a time to develop any meaningful genetic character by inbreeding.

4. Because the definition of inferiority resorted to is itself restricted in terms of the characteristics of human beings, that is, the instruments and tests used are assumed to measure genetically determined characteristics in groups that can be compared to other groups without significant overlap. The evidence is clearly against that. Also, the assumption is that if one consistently and positively modifies the experience of deprived groups, this modification will not be reflected in significant improvement. There is no evidence to prove this closed-end theory of environmental influences.

The fact is that the limits of environmental effect on intelligence have not been ascertained. Even under the most controlled conditions, tests of human beings in a racist society cannot eliminate the flagrant and subtle influences that permeate every aspect of American life. Even the pre-birth environment would need to be controlled, for the damage to urban infants whose mothers are deprived of adequate health care and nutrition, of psychological security, and of self-respect, cannot be fully ascertained. Until the conditions of life of American Negroes are in all respects equal to those available to others, no valid test of genetic capacity can be devised. Such conditions of equality must be achieved as speedily as possible.

The ambiguity of the concept of race was first raised by Franz Boas and Ruth Benedict in the 1930s, and the ambiguity of the American Negro as a racial entity was raised by Otto Klineberg in the late 1930s. The ambiguity of the phenomena to be measured and the limits of the instruments and the definition of the group must be as rigorously questioned today.

There is today a growing and persistent counterattack among biologists, psychologists, and social scientists against the neo-racist intellectual backlash. Further, more vigorous attention to the social responsibilities of social science is leading a number of scholars, particularly among the young, into an overt role in the struggle for positive social change. Objectivity and pure science are now perceived by a growing number to be consistent with, and not antithetical to, social responsibility. They are perceived to be appropriate, though limited, in themselves, but monstrous when taken to mean that conditions of injustice must not touch the spirit or motivate a man to act.

The involvement of social scientists in the *Brown* decision set social science and the law on a common path. There can be no turning from it.

BLACK NATIONALISM: A VERIFICATION OF THE
NEGATIVE CONSEQUENCES OF SEGREGATION

In 1954 when the *Brown* decision was handed down, desegregation and integration were the priority of the civil rights movement and Negroes generally. A decade later, many militants proclaimed the death of the civil rights movement and denied the value of integration itself, and specifically questioned the significance of the *Brown* decision and the truth of the social science findings on which it rested. One must thus look at the decision and its social science foundation from a new perspective and inquire whether these charges are justified.

During the years since 1954, black nationalism experienced a sharp rise in support from young Negro militants and from many whites. This represents in some forms the continuation of the nationalism of the Garvey movement of the 1920s, identifiable in degree by the black nationalism of Malcolm X. In other, and more serious, manifestations it has gained support among Negro students and youth. The seeming common denomination of both is the repudiation of integration and the apparent repudiation of the struggle for desegregation, the rejection of the *Brown* decision, and the implicit rejection of the whole rationale and psychological approach to the meaning of racism. This would logically include a denial of the social science explanation of the inevitability of inferiority in segregated systems on which the *Brown* decision depended.

Under the guise of assuming a positive identity, black nationalism has adopted an imitation of white racism with its deification of race, its attempt to make a virtue out of color, its racist mystique. This rationale argues that the detrimental consequences of a biracial society are neutralized or transformed into positive consequences by virtue of the fact that Negroes themselves are now asserting the value of racism. This argument would give primary weight to voluntarism, that is, that racism would lead to affirmative not negative results if it is voluntarily accepted or sought by the former victims as it was voluntarily maintained by the oppressors. The character of racism would depend on the attitude one had toward it; it would have no objective reality of its own. Consistent with certain contemporary philosophical positions, the nature of reality and of ethical judgment about separatism would be governed not by objectively determined evidence or by consequences but by the subjective view.

In 1954, on the contrary, it would have been the consensus in the Negro and white liberal communities that white racism would have gained its greatest triumph had it been able to persuade its Negro victims that segregation was not only acceptable but desirable in itself, and that the justification for this separatism was color alone.

The paranoia of racism, whether imposed or sought, must rest on insecurity. It is the verification of the psychological interpretation of the negative consequences of segregation. Racism does produce doubts and insecurities in the victims as well as in the perpetrators. It increases hostility and aggression and self-hatred. Actually, the present separatist movement, the present intensity of the cult—though one must still question whether it reflects the position of the majority of Negroes—is certainly fashionable in terms of treatment given by the press, television, and publishing. The semantics has been effectively changed in an abrupt few years. Many, even most, Negroes and most white liberals in positions requiring public articulateness, as well as many moderate newspapers, have substituted the word "black" for "Negro," however awkward it may sound to them—some from the conviction that the one represents liberation and the other submission; but many out of dread of the unfashionable and of the pejorative judgment of black militants, who have mounted a campaign of verbal condemnation and threat against those whites and blacks who resist. The chief function of the use of the term "black" now is to demonstrate that one is identified with the new militant thrust. (The new elite includes a highly select group of converted or contributing whites.) It is regarded as offering a basis for differentiating between the truly anointed among Negroes who will reserve for themselves the designation *blacks,* a test of racial loyalty consigning all middle-class Uncle Toms to the damnable category of *Negro.* It could be argued persuasively and with reason—if reason too is not now to be repudiated or considered too middle-class—that the term "black" adds to the confusion of America's racial dilemma. Certainly it is not an African term. Like Negro, it, too, is a "white man's" term. It is Anglo-Saxon, while Negro is Latin and, more recently, Spanish in origin. Not long ago it was considered militant to insist that newspapers capitalize the term "Negro."

The most serious new dimension to the new form of black nationalism is not the threat of violence which it poses for white society—a threat which is for the most part verbal and after the fact—but the very real threat which it presents to middle-class and middle-class-aspiring Negroes. Some of the most incoherently articulate spokesmen seem to be more intensely and fervently anti-middle-class-educated-Negro than they are antiwhite. While some advocates or interpreters of the Black Power movement are middle-class themselves—professors, college students, white and Negro clergymen—many of its advocates are dominated by deep feelings of racial self-hatred. Part of the pattern of pretense and posturing includes a suicidal eagerness to ascribe all middle-class patterns of speech, grammar, dress, manners, and style of life to whites, while reserving for the exclusive use of Negroes the uncouth and the vulgar. This is garden-variety racism at its most obscene—and no less so because it is now being sold by Negroes rather than by whites. Some racial "militants" have accepted the white man's negative stereotype of the Negro. It was not acceptable when fostered by white oppression; it cannot be acceptable in the guise of flamboyant black militancy.

This Lorelei quest for identity is based on superstition. Despite the verbal transformation from self-contempt to apparent pride, the conditions of injustice remain. We are asked to obscure them by the rhetorical posturing of pride. In a strikingly similar analogy, it is psychologically obvious that any man who proclaims how irresistible and potent and virile he is must have deep doubts about it. He would clearly be regarded as preoccupied with sexual anxiety. Such self-pretense conceals—or attempts to conceal—deep, poignant, and tragic insecurity. Given the fact that the realities of racism in America have not changed, and that the Negro is still condemned to segregated schools, to segregated and deteriorated residential areas, and to an economic role which is not competitive with the white society, the cult of blackness must be recognized as what it is—a ritualized denial of anguished despair and resentment of the failure of society to meet its promises.

Separatism is an attempt to create verbal realities as substitutes for social, political, and economic realities. It is another and intense symptom of the psychological damage which a racist society inflicts on its victims.

A specific indication of the damage of separatism is that the victims internalize racism. Some forms of black separatism involve genuine and deep self-destructive suicidal dynamics. They reflect the most cruel, barbaric, tragic, dehumanizing consequences of white oppression—the wish of the oppressed to die—and in dying to destroy others in a similar predicament. The white racists who so damage their fellow human beings must be prepared to face the same judgment which the Nazis who sent millions to death camps must face.

Whatever the motivation for individuals associated with the black nationalist movement, I consider the movement as a whole to be sick, regressive, and tyrannical. It is anti-intellectual. Its main source of energy is emotionalism rather than thought.

Responding to a button reading "Being Black Is Not Enough," several Negroes said, "Well, being white has always been enough." But if one looks at the moral decay, the instability, and the unresolved problems of white society, one perceives that being white is not enough, that it is effective only in terms of self-aggrandizement and at the expense of exploitation of those who are not white. Its success depends on victimization, for racism is not only subjective, it also demands an object. Positive racism has the necessary obverse of rejection of those who do not meet the chosen racial criteria.

So, rather than refuting the social science assumptions that led to the *Brown* decision, the present cult of black separatism verifies them intensely. Black separatism can be seen as a "sour-grapes and sweet-lemon" reaction against the failure of the society to implement and enforce the findings of *Brown*.

This vocal, well-publicized, well-endowed cult has to be understood for what it is, for otherwise it can be cynically manipulated and used by white racists who are now the often silent allies of the separatists. The rationale of the sophisticated white intellectual who endorses black separatism in his university, his church, his political party, his academic or professional society, while continuing to live in a restricted suburb and continuing to support the institutional relegation of Negroes to inferior status, must be seen by Negroes for what it is, an attempt to handle racial ambivalence, to deal with guilt.

The basic standard for such understanding is that which functioned in the *Brown* decision, namely that racism and segregation are a reflection of superstition, institutionalized untruth, cruelty, and injustice, and that race is irrelevant as a criterion for preference or rejection. The poignant tragedy is that the society is using the victimized groups as the agent for the perpetuation of irreconcilable injustice and racial irrelevance. Any white or black intellectual who denies this must be more comfortable with superstition and rationalization. One cannot deal with the reorganization of society on a nonracial basis by intensifying racist symptoms.

Separatists tend to substitute rhetorical satisfactions of reiterated pride of race for confrontation of racist injustice. They rarely address themselves to immediate specific programs designed to reorganize society, but rather comfort themselves with grandiose ideology, "black awareness" campaigns, and long-range plans such as demands for separatist states or back-to-Africa movements. They seldom invest their energies in attempts to abolish deteriorated housing or deteriorated education. Black nationalism is the easier way.

Neither do poor white racists address themselves to specific problems, such as inadequate nutrition and the life chances of their children. Rather, they are caught up in the semantics of white superiority. Neither poor whites nor blacks can ever change the conditions of their lives as long as they remain so narcotized. Racists, white and black, are essentially hopeless people who have given up on the possibilities of justice and on their own capacity to further justice.

It is fashionable also among whites to defend black separatism to other whites not on its merits, as they may do in the company of Negroes, but as a necessary step toward eventual integration, as a "phase" restless Negroes must go through. Indeed, some black separatists offer the same self-defeating rationale. Yet, at the end of the nineteenth century in the post-Reconstruction period, institutionalized segregation was also explained as a "phase" by whites and blacks who argued that it was a necessary first stage to prepare Negroes for inclusion into society. Instead, such racism became institutionalized and rigid, and then was explained and defended for its own sake as a desirable way of life. In American society, segregation—and separatism, which is the same thing semantically disguised and camouflaged by self-acceptance—tends to be self-perpetuating rather than self-neutralizing.

Nor can one build a solid pride on the quicksands of emotion, anger, rage, hatred—no matter how justifiable. Genuine pride—the pride that makes life worth the struggle with some hope of serenity—must come from solid personal achievement, from sensitivity and concern and respect for one's fellow man, from compassion and the willingness to struggle to give some substance to one's own life by trying to help others live with confidence in the possibility of positives. Pride, like humility, is destroyed by one's insistence that he possesses it.

Racism in any form is dangerous, but particularly, as is now true among many whites and Negroes, when it is intellectually supported. Such supporters often fail to follow the implication of their rhetoric to its logical conclusion—that if segregation and separatism are desirable and good as a phase, and as a means, they are even more to be desired as ends in themselves.

All the implications of the *Brown* decision and all the social science arguments in its support point to the inherent dangers of racism. The latest surge toward self-imposed separatism is the greatest verification of all. I read into the separatist movement among Negroes a more severe symptom than those described in *Brown*. It convinces me even more persuasively that social scientists, as others, must redouble our efforts to obliterate racism whatever its manifestations, wherever it appears. The failures of the desegregation movement are not evidence that social science involvement was a mistake; rather they are evidence that the phenomenon to be studied—racism—and the social policies necessary to eradicate it are far more complex and difficult to understand and to implement than social scientists had previously believed.

6

SOCIAL CRITIC
OR
SOCIAL APOLOGIST?

THE NATIONAL PREOCCUPATION with the Watergate scandal
has carried the seeds of danger that we might reach, through
overexposure, a point of diminishing concern with the
fundamental moral and ethical issues inherent in this new
reminder of Lord Acton's analysis of the corruptive aspects
of power, aided and abetted by intellectuals, generally, and
social scientists, in particular. Prolonged exposure to systematic and planned immorality at the highest level of government is an experience that staggers the imagination and
confounds reason, and, thus, is so incredible as to demand
escape from confrontation. This admittedly merciful, adaptive search for stabilization in the face of extreme pressure is
disturbing, for it would bring relief at the cost of sensitivity
and responsiveness.

The fundamental problems posed by a Watergate are age-
old and universal. Man has been unable to employ power
and control over his fellow man with an optimum balance of
clarity and compassion; he has been unable to resist the

temptation to abuse power through mindless egocentricity. When partial power seeks to become absolute, insatiable lust for power seems to lead relentlessly to corruption, to the use of power not as an instrument of social good but rather as an end in itself. The quest for power is contaminated when insecure and fragile human beings insist upon absolute affirmations and upon absolute power without regard to means. The inevitable consequences of the unchecked political power lust must be authoritarianism and tyranny.

Limited options are available to restrain the more devastating abuses of power. The framers of the American Constitution relied upon the checks and balances of a tripartite form of government to counter unfettered power. The Bill of Rights protected both the freedom of the press to serve as an unfettered monitor of government and the freedom of the individual to think, to speak, and to dissent, as critically important checks on abuses of governmental power.

But, despite such controls, the Watergate phenomenon of break-ins, electronic surveillance, the misuse of governmental law enforcement agencies—the Justice Department, the Federal Bureau of Investigation, the mysterious CIA, and other probably more mysterious intelligence apparatus —has demonstrated how effectively governmental power can be used to subvert its primary constructive purpose of protecting the rights and interests of its citizens. Watergate has made clear how deeply government abuse of the people has permeated all levels of government—local, state, and federal—obliterating any genuine distinction between our practice of democratic government and the functional reality of an authoritarian system. Still, it would be misleading to overemphasize Watergate as the American sickness, in spite of the fact that the Watergate disclosures so far reveal

[121]

a pattern of perfidy among elected and appointed federal governmental officials that goes beyond adequate description by the terms "political corruption" or even "organized crime." For the first time in American history, the American people have been confronted with American governmental power itself as the source of, the architect of, and the director of a pervasive pattern of criminal activity. But, Watergate can be understood only as the most recent intense symptom and as a culmination of the historical dynamics of the pervasive sickness inherent in the American political, economic, and social system. The seriousness of the Watergate revelations is in the possibility that the depth and intensity of this latest symptom might be indicative of a grave prognosis—that the sickness of the American system has reached the threshold of a terminal social and national disease. Watergate is the democratization of evil in America. Negroes had always known that our government is oppressive. Watergate, thus, makes "niggers" of us all.

Watergate tells us only what we already knew—that America is seriously ill. Watergate highlights the complexity of the American illness, for these crimes were planned and committed by successful—not overtly disadvantaged—Americans who daily preached about the importance of preserving the American democratic way of life. They preached about "law and order" even as they pandered to the prejudices and exploited the ignorance of the majority of the American electorate for political success. These were pragmatic men who themselves were symbols of the success of the upward mobility promises of America. These were men who boasted about their own virtue and sneered at the frailties of less successful human beings as they flaunted their friendships with such affluent and successful religious

leaders as Billy Graham and Norman Vincent Peale. These
were men who were dominated by an insatiable hunger for
power and domination as values which must take precedence over elementary decency, justice, humanity, love, and
truth. These men demonstrated by their acts the depth of
their frustrations, the pathetic emptiness within them, the
futility of seeking affirmation of the value and quality of the
self through material acquisitions and the endless pursuit of
power. These men demonstrated the frightening superficiality of American culture and the awesome deficiencies of
American education.

These men are Americans.

These men are very sick.

The enormity of human culpability of Watergate could
not have occurred without the acquiescence of significant
groups of the American citizenry. Watergate must be understood in the context of a society in which a vast majority of
the American middle class, working class, and economic,
social, and intellectual elites have knowingly bargained
away their fundamental values, ideals, rights, and liberties,
to political officials who promised to reward their greed and
pandered to their primitive passions and prejudices. Those
government officials who have been under the Watergate
spotlight were the same architects of the manipulation of
American prejudices that employed such code words as
"busing," "quotas," "law and order" as thinly disguised
semantics for the cruel superstition of racism, a verbal exploitation of the superstitions and rationalizations of the
populace that opened the way to the most recent rationalization for government venality, "national security."

Euphemistic distortions of the fundamental moral concerns of man must be understood as a consequence of

pervasive failures of our educational system to prepare human beings to use reason and intelligence as an integral part of ethical standards. Educational institutions, under the guise of realism, continue to act as if their role and function is to reflect prevailing immoralities and to train human minds to accept and understand euphemistic verbal covers for effective social and political immorality and their inequities. They seem, for the most part, to place a high intellectual value on moral relativism, on moral detachment, and on those virtues which are empirically validated by personal success and prestige. In spite of the Watergates of the past, in spite of the extreme barbarity of Nazism, in spite of the mindless cruelty of Vietnam, most prestigious intellectuals and educational institutions still dare to justify their abrogation of moral obligation and leadership on the grounds of intellectual sophistication. It is my judgment that this is a rationalization which seeks to obscure the fact that the pose of moral detachment provides for the alleged intellectual social scientists a safe and protective haven and the necessary flexibility for the use of intelligence and training in the service of power and tyranny; or, at best, provides acceptance of flagrant forms of inequality and injustice in their society.

Yet, the intellectual, the academician, and the social scientist, in a democracy, have a special responsibility—an obligation—to play the role of social critic in the face of such rationalization. As Machiavelli wrote, the role of social critic is not likely to be rewarded. He said:

It must be considered that there is nothing more difficult to carry out, nor more doubtful of success, nor more dangerous to handle, than to initiate a new order of things. For the reformer has enemies in all those who profit from the old order, and only lukewarm defenders in all those who would profit by the new order, this lukewarmness arising partly from fear of their adversaries, who have the laws in their favour; and partly from the incredulity of mankind, who do not truly believe in anything new until they have had actual experience of it. . . .

SOCIAL SCIENTISTS AS INTELLECTUAL MERCENARIES

Even the most intelligent of human beings can be seduced and purchased by the lure, the glamour, and the glitter of power. It is not difficult to understand how social scientists themselves can be deflected from their obligatory role of social critic into the safer role of social apologist.

Probably the dominant influence on the social scientist as social critic was the Lockean radical view of man and society, based upon a form of environmentalism tied necessarily to Locke's literalistic concept of the equality of man. In his aggressive assertion of his concern for human equality, Locke established the intellectual basis and theory for modern social science and provided what proved to be the radical rationale for political revolutions—the philosophical basis of Jeffersonian democracy and the fundamental and specific rationale for the American, French, and Russian revolutions. Yet, the Lockean radical social philosophy did not progress in a straight line but was blocked and diverted by retrogressions in social thought that persisted through the past three centuries. The doctrines of instinctivism, theories of inherent inferiority and biological superiority of certain races, the persistent infection of literal Darwinism in social thought, such as William Graham Sumner's insistence on the right of the strong to dominate the weak, contaminated social philosophy. Social theorists and social scientists returned to the role of social apologists, abandoning the more risky roles of social criticism and social action.

But, at the rise of twentieth-century social science, particularly in American behaviorism and the Pavlovian psychology of the Soviet Union, the dominant theme emerging was a curious return to seventeenth-century Lockean environmentalism and egalitarianism. Social scientists were inescapably required to resume the role of social critic. In the field of psychology the fundamental assumptions of behaviorists like Watson and Skinner must be understood in terms of the ability of man to modify human behavior through controlling the social and political environment. Certainly, in the work of such social anthropologists as Franz Boas and Ruth Benedict as they influenced the social psychology of Otto Klineberg; and the contributions of such giants in American sociology as Louis Wirth, Charles S. Johnson, E. Franklin Frazier; and the pioneer work of Gunnar Myrdal, the role of social critic was resumed. Their contributions led inevitably to the historic *Brown* decision of the United States Supreme Court in May of 1954; and to its footnote eleven citing those social scientists who dared to be social critics, who dared to be unapologetic exponents of social justice—and who rejected the silent or active role of defenders of the status quo.

One would have expected that with the stamp of acceptance provided by the highest judicial body in the United States the role of social scientists as social critics would have been reinforced and that the role of social scientists as apologists of the status quo would have been demeaned. But events during the past decade, and particularly during the past five years, again demonstrated that social progress is not positively linear. It has now become not only respectable but also rewarding for certain other social scientists to yield to the most seductive temptation of all: the acceptance of the role of intellectual mercenaries—to use their training, their theory, their verbal skills, and their computers as instruments in the perpetuation of prevailing political power, in the pay of those defenders of the status quo who reward their social scientists well in publicity, prestige, and proximity to power. Most social scientists have surrendered to the contrary temptation; retreating to the sterilities and trivia of the past, they tend to remain detached, deliberately uninvolved in the problems of social justice and social change, safe from controversy and protected from being accused of availability for hire.

The human deterioration of the privileged has not been adequately discussed by social scientists and philosophers. The failure to come to grips with this core problem reflects many things, among them the fact that those who write about the problems of our cities are more likely to identify themselves with the privileged than with the victims of human insensitivity.

Within the past decade it has become fashionable for a group of social scientists, fortified by their training and trappings and jargon and methodological pretensions, to reverse the direction of the Allport, Boas, Bunche, Klineberg, Myrdal models of social science and express as a virtue their alliance with the present controllers of social and political power. The present group of neo-conservative social scientists are well-publicized defenders of the political, social, racial, and economic status quo. These social scientists write learned treatises demonstrating that the problems of the urban disadvantaged and other oppressed groups in our society reflect essentially the deficiencies of those who are victimized. The victims are to be blamed for the victimization, either through their inferior genes, their "cultural deprivation," or their environmentally or biologically determined tendencies toward vandalism, crime, and violence. It is economically and socially profitable now for a small group of social scientists, with their bases at prestigious universities, to offer social science as a tool for moral and ethical indifference toward the plight of the poor and to use their prestige to justify continued inequities. They argue aggressively that institutional changes will not bring about any positive changes in the education of minorities; that desegregation of the schools is a snare and a delusion—if not utopian; that ethnic and racial distinctions and inequities are irremediable or that attempts to remedy them would create more problems than the present injustices. I offer this as evidence of the subtle but profound form of human degradation.

Social scientists, who by their glib, fatuous willingness to compromise the fundamental humanity of dark-skinned children and who by doing so provide public officials with rationalizations for regressive policies of malignant neglect, are not only accessories to the perpetuation of injustices, they become indistinguishable from the active agents of injustice. This role raises the serious question of whether social scientists and the type of research for which they are responsible should be permitted to have any direct role in decisions on important matters of equity, justice, and equality among groups of human beings. Christopher Jencks himself asserts that "Academic opinion has vacillated from one side to the other, according to the political mood of the times." This observation is disturbingly true—although there were no indications that Jencks and his associates were disturbed by this fact and its implications. They did not seem to understand that in this role of follower of the "political mood" social scientists are indistinguishable from politicians. And certainly they then tend to become dependent upon the politicians for small consultant favors or public exposure, and seemingly for political influence. Under these conditions social scientists, in spite of their scientific pretensions, are no more dependable in the quest for social justice than are other citizens. What should be their primary allegiance in the tortuous quest for truth is subtly subordinated to the temptation to seek power, fame, and political influence. They then, in effect, become politicians, using scientific jargon, methodology, and computers in an attempt to disguise their essentially political role—a disguise facilitated by identification with a prestigious academic institution.

At the risk of seeming to be personal and resorting to ad hominem argument, I would like to describe the dominant and publicized social science pattern of this period as the Moynihan Era. The Moynihan Era might be characterized as an era in which certain social scientists, those who are most widely publicized, offer themselves as agents of those who are in political power. Some accept positions in government with the understanding that they will be resident liberals, social scientists whose main responsibility will be to explain or apologize for the actions of those who wield political and economic power. By their training, their style, their language, they are particularly effective in influencing the opinions of the intellectual and academic communities.

They have had additional responsibilities for rationalizing political decisions which seek to maintain inequities, inequality, and cruelties under such catch-phrases as "benign neglect" or with the assertion that we do not know enough to change clearly unjust practices; they seek to make intolerable and clearly destructive inequities palatable. Under the cover of prestigious academic institutions they have ample, if not monopolistic, access to government consultantships, foundation grants, and widespread media coverage. Some individuals, such as Daniel P. Moynihan himself, will be flagrant and direct in their for-hire role in exchange for rewards of prestige, publicity, and power. Others, such as Jensen, Banfield, Forrester, Armor, and Jencks will be more indirect. Still others, such as Bell and Glazer, will be more subtle and polysyllabic apologists for the status quo.

The common denominator among this new breed of social science mercenaries is that they have supplanted the optimism, the drive for social change of the social scientists of the Allport era with their use of social science as a weapon for the maintenance of things-as-they-are. They align themselves with those with power and against the aspirations of the powerless victims of flagrant and subtle social inequities. They argue that this is evidence of their tough-mindedness and objectivity and establishes their claim to scientific validity.

Without question the right of these individuals to express their personal opinions and to seek to influence social policy should be safeguarded and defended to the utmost—freedom to think and to communicate are unqualifiable rights in a democratic and academic society. Social scientists like all other citizens cannot be denied their constitutional right to seek to influence policy and decisions. Nor can the issue of the subordination of the pursuit of truth to the practical problems of political reality be raised only in regard to certain social scientists. Educators, clergymen, and those social scientists whose political values one identifies with must also be required to meet the test of pursuit of truth.

Freedom of speech and inquiry must be preserved and protected for all citizens in a democracy—and certainly these rights must be protected for social scientists without regard to their particular social biases. However, those rights, when exercised by social scientists should not and must not be confused with their role and obligations as social scientists. When individual social scientists or groups of social scientists are operating as paid apologists for politicians, or when they are exponents of rights and interests of special-interest groups, when they are expressing their primary identification with particular segments of society, and when they are understandably concerned with enhancing and protecting their personal safety and prestige and with increasing their power, and when these goals are given precedence over the primary concern and loyalty that social scientists must have in the search for truth and justice, then these realities must be made clear. Individuals trained in social science cannot be permitted to use the raiments of social science as a disguise for their personal quest for power. The dangers of this amoral use of human intelligence are associated with a perversion of the meaning of objectivity in social science; they are an integral part of the use of human intelligence as an effective instrument in the subtle and flagrant forms of political and social corruption.

When social scientists are operating in the important areas of social justice and equity they can claim no special immunity to intense critical scrutiny of their findings, particularly when those findings have clear policy implications. In fact, it is precisely in regard to their policy impact that the findings and interpretations of social scientists must be subjected to the most rigorous critical analysis. In these areas of social justice and equity the contributions of social scientists can be accepted only as one of the many considerations to be taken into account in arriving at policy decisions. Even with a methodology which seeks to assure a higher degree of objectivity in arriving at an understanding of social dynamics, social scientists cannot justifiably claim to be immune from class and racial biases which distort their interpretations.

A quiet and pervasive danger inherent in the subordinate power role of social scientists is that in seeking to develop and use techniques designed to influence military, governmental, and other "practical" leaders, social scientists might be tempted to make subtle or flagrant compromises with positive human values or truth. Social scientists are human. They, like other human beings, are titillated by power—are susceptible to the rationalizations that seek to justify a variety of accommodations and compromises which make them acceptable to, tolerated, and rewarded by those who wield the primary power in society. Social scientists have been socialized in the same societies as other human beings. Like other human beings, they may be receptive to the same influences—both explicit and subtle—of the groups with which they identify or those groups or individuals whom they perceive as having determinative power. In making their adjustments to these social realities they, like other human beings, are frequently required, consciously or unconsciously, to subordinate their loyalties to intellectual rigor, rational and moral thought, empiricism, if not truth, in order to protect themselves from ridicule, exclusion, and direct or indirect retaliation. These are problems which cannot be ignored. At this period in human history, these problems cannot be resolved or minimized by self-righteous denials or repression. Any attempt to avoid facing and positively resolving these dilemmas can only be at the price of a continued academic impotence and irresponsibility of social science.

To avoid the dangers of social science collusion with those who control political and economic power in our society, the public must be alerted to the vulnerabilities—the human frailties—of social scientists. There must be continued reliance upon the political, the legislative, and the judicial apparatuses—in spite of their imperfections—for determinations on matters of equity and justice. These democratic processes cannot be permitted to be eroded, no matter how subtly, by a social science posture of omniscience.

THE ROLE OF SOCIAL CRITIC
AND DIAGNOSTICIAN

Because of clear and present dangers, particularly disturbing in a nuclear age, in a volatile period of tortuous transition from accepted injustice throughout the world toward some higher level of social morality, one cannot permit contemporary social scientists to be social apologists with impunity. Social scientists must be controlled by the willingness of the intellectual community to assume and act upon the risk of exposing the use of social science for social apology. Social science professional associations must monitor the activities of social scientists in matters affecting social policy. They must develop just and fair techniques for continuous, severe examinations of research, theories, and

[133]

findings of social scientists; and certainly they must develop effective methods for alerting an indifferent or gullible public and for protecting that public from the pretensions of scientific infallibility, and from the consequences of prostituted social science.

All of this must be done within the framework of that due regard to freedom of inquiry and respect for the right of individuals to differ, and certainly with unqualified adherence to fundamental human and democratic processes. But there must be vigilance; intellectual vigilance is essential to the expansion and preservation of human dignity. In assuming this highly specific social critic role the social scientist must be intellectually, morally, and personally unafraid. An intimidated intellectual is an inherent self-contradiction. The guiding principle of the concerned and courageous social critic must be the dictum of Herbert Spencer: "The profoundest of all infidelities is the fear that the truth will be bad."

The social critic must attempt to be as precise and as objective as possible in determining whether behavioral patterns and characteristics are more nonadaptive than adaptive; more destructive than constructive; more irrational and randomly aggressive than rational, thoughtful, and empathic; and whether a group or individual seems consistently more preoccupied with power and its expansion as ends in themselves than concerned with power as means toward the attainment of the constructive goals of justice, social sensitivity, and empathy.

Ironically, in even the most "sick" societies and nations there are a few individuals who do not share all of the symptoms of that society in which they have been socialized and of which they are a part, who for unknown reasons seem compelled to react against some of the more obviously destructive symptoms of their group; and an even smaller number who will assume the risky roles of overt dissent, reacting against the more flagrant and inhumane symptoms of sickness in their society.

It is not easy to understand the motivation and determinants of such overt dissenters. They were subject to the same educational, institutional, and coercive family and community pressures that determine the attitudes, values, and behavior patterns of normal human beings in their society; but, nonetheless, they reject the socialized conformity behavior accepted by the majority and they rebel against what they believe to be a pattern of sickness of their society.

The critical social diagnostician who assumes the further role of overt social critic and social therapist without question assumes these roles at the risk of loss of status, personal alienation, group rejection, coercion, ridicule, punishment, and, at times, death. A truly reflective social critic must also run the more disturbing risk of assuming these roles and possible punishments without certainty that his diagnosis is accurate, and with the related anxiety that his adversaries may be more realistic, more practical, and more effective. It is a social fact that the symptoms of social illness diagnosed by one observer can readily be accepted as social norms and given validity as the accepted folkways and mores of the society as a whole. The accepted rationalizations of a given society establish a pragmatic validity for the prevailing patterns of social behavior.

Traditionally, societies have sought to prevent their erosion by dissenters, who may be seen and treated as dogmatists, by imposing upon such individuals restraints, regulations, and other forms of coercive control, procedures and practices justified on the grounds of maintaining social stability and effectiveness. It is difficult for the thoughtful social diagnostician to differentiate his role from that of the social critic and from that of the social dissenter. And it is clearly difficult for those who control the power of a given society to differentiate the role of the social diagnostician, critic, and dissenter from that of the traitor.

Not infrequently a social system confronted with persistent social diagnosticians and dissenters seeks to protect itself from these threats by blaming the diagnosticians for the undeniable symptoms and the increased severity of the illness of the social system. But, despite persistent hostility and even repression, throughout American history there have been dissenters—a minority of intellectuals, priests, lawyers, members of the Supreme Court, minority-group leadership, young people, and concerned citizens—who have insisted upon a more literal interpretation and implementation of the American Bill of Rights. They have played a major role in balancing the more pragmatic, realistic, negative symptoms of the American illness. Unlike the majority of their fellow citizens they do not seem to have lost the capacity for outrage—they do not seem to be easily intimidated and it does not seem to be easy to silence or destroy them. They have contributed to the functional stabilization of the American society and they have bargained for and obtained the needed time in which progression toward the health of the society could be achieved.

7

OMBUDSMEN FOR SOCIETY

PSYCHOLOGY IS BASIC to all systematic attempts to understand the nature of man. Psychology is the arrogance of human intellect that leads man to validate his claim to uniqueness by asking questions about his own identity, by demanding or creating answers. It is the convergence of ideas through which man seeks to deify himself and to justify his sacredness; yet, it mocks and taunts him with fears and anxieties, driving him to seek resolution and affirmation.

Psychology is the source of human curiosity and creativity—that is, of intelligence—and of the insatiable, self-perpetuating cycle of introspection and action. It seeks a systematic understanding of man's dynamic interaction with his environment. Psychologists must concern themselves with the totality of man—man the animal, man the social being; man the victim of uncontrollable forces but, as architect and engineer, the master of forces not previously controlled; man the god, and the worshipper of gods; man the lonely being, the gregarious being; man the creative being, who seeks to give meaning and substance to the illusive chimera of the human ego. It is the human predicament that the ego has no indigenous substance. The self is determined by the external—by experience—by manipulation of that environment to meet its needs. The biological and physical sciences must take into account the complexity and pathos of the human brain and its search to understand the perceivable and conceivable environment and to devise instruments that may reduce threats to life and give substance to existence.

Psychology is the core of the social sciences—history, economics, political science, sociology. It unifies and gives coherence of meaning to the humanities. It is central to religion's struggle for moral understanding and to philosophy's search for rational understanding and control. It is implicit in literature's exploration of human motivation, its frailties and its grandeur, in its attempts to communicate human feelings and experience. Art, architecture, and engineering, the planning and building of villages and cities and nations, and the dreams of new towns and utopias are the objectification of human thought and aspiration.

I believe that it is the business of the psychologist, as it is the business of all social scientists, to be concerned with the totality of man and with the health, the stability, and the effectiveness of the human society as a whole. To constrict concern is to be intellectually and scientifically irresponsible. I believe that the science of the study of man must seek systematic understanding and control—in the positive sense—of human behavior. Psychology must be a value-laden science, and the fundamental value which must sustain it is a concern with the welfare of man. A social scientist cannot be indifferent to the destiny and the predicament of man and society any more than medicine could have been indifferent to plagues and disease. The social scientist must be committed to social change. There is no pure, indifferent, nontechnologically oriented use of disciplined human intelligence in social science, and there is room for none.

In the present curious set of turbulence and change in status relationships among human beings—economic, racial, caste, national—confusion and chaos are endemic, without regard to ideology. Unwillingness to use immoral means to attain allegedly moral ends has been a casualty; another casualty is reason. But now the world seems to demand that disciplined intelligence and reason seek rational answers to problems of injustice and human meaning, that such matters no longer be left to religion. When I was a graduate student in psychology at Columbia University, my professors, whom I loved, persistently cautioned me against too obvious a moralistic approach to psychology. They warned that my moralism would interfere with my being a top-rate scientist. I was, by virtue of my cultural deprivation, somewhat perplexed, but even then I thought that the goal of psychology was to seek to legitimize and systematize morality among men. It was explained to me patiently and carefully that this was not the business of science, that what I assumed to be the task of science—concern with kindness, love, and humanity—was not. And psychology, above all, had to be a science.

And I would say, "If it is not the business of psychology, what is it the business of?" And they would smile and say, "Philosophy. Those kinds of abstractions belong to the philosophers and the religious men."

That was in 1937, 1938, 1939. I revolted against it then, although I was realistic enough not to pursue it rigorously with my professors. I remained preoccupied with how science could help man solve problems of social responsibility and social justice. When I began to teach at the College of the City of New York in 1940, the psychology and philosophy departments, which had been one and the same, were separated. I recall vividly the sense of achievement projected by my friends and colleagues in the psychology department as they told me they were now free and independent of philosophy. There were elaborate plans to build laboratories; department meeting after department meeting was devoted to allocation of the budget for the purchasing of instruments and machines. We at City College were part of the accelerated momentum to demonstrate that psychology had the same status as the physical sciences. The methods and the semantics of nineteenth-century physics became the early symbols of psychology's new scientific status. The fact that psychological problems are rooted in the biology and physiology of the organism stimulated the growth of psychology as a natural science; its status was higher, therefore, than that of social science. Psychology's claim to be a precise, empirical science that could hold its own at least in academic debates and in competition for limited funds seemed justified and reinforced by the power and influence of American pragmatism with its impatience with theorizing, and by American behaviorism and Watsonianism. We gleefully opened the doors to our new laboratories. We bought more white coats and white rats.

These empirical claims were countered early by Freudianism, which disturbingly explored the nonrational and the deeper recesses of the human psyche. It is still difficult to deal with such complexities with "scientific precision" as this is defined by the imitation of physics. Another counterforce was social psychology, which incorrigibly and exasperatingly refused to be constrained by instruments and insisted upon trying to deal with or trying to define the intricate phenomena of human social interaction.

Gestalt and organismic perspectives sought to reconcile the claims and pretensions of laboratory psychology with psychological realities, but just as psychology appeared to have won its right to be called a science, just as we were proudly exhibiting our white rats, abrupt revolutions in physics and biology rocked the scientific world. The literal and figurative explosions in Los Alamos, Hiroshima, and Nagasaki, the awesome realities of the nuclear age demanded redefinitions of science, of ideology, of war, of the use of power in imposing one's will upon others. The nuclear age made it inconceivable that science and values be separated again. As I read *The Bulletin of Atomic Scientists,* I found that physicists were capable of guilt; they expressed an anguished plea to mankind to understand that science as they had defined it and, ironically, as they had demonstrated its success, could also be a horror. They could no longer be "objective." We found that anguish personified in Einstein (who, I believe, committed suicide either actually or psychologically). We found the anguish in Russell, in Oppenheimer, Pauling, and others.

There were intensified demands that human intelligence be used to increase the chances of human survival and to reduce the imminent possibility of total destruction. The anxiety of the atomic scientists led to a rejection of the role of dispassionate experimentation and, without apology, they assumed the difficult role of attempting to influence public policy to see that their discoveries would be used for the benefit of mankind. So, also, other groups of citizens, students, minorities, and oppressed peoples throughout the world clamored for social justice. Those who were believed to have the power to control the destiny of their fellow man were to be required to assume the responsibility of that power.

The nuclear age brought with it social revolutions; economic and class and racial injustices could no longer be quietly accepted; they could no longer be imposed, and they could no longer be sustained by military power. The stakes had become ultimate. A major restructuring of social systems would be necessary if mankind were to survive. Even ideology had to be subordinated to fundamental values of the preservation of man.

The psychologists' pretensions of scientific exactness were revealed as an absurdity. Our brass instruments and white rats were part of a serene and archaic world of the ancient history of the nineteenth and early twentieth centuries. The physicists and the biologists were crying for help, but we insisted on defining our science in their terms and we could not help them. Because we so uncritically rejected values, and philosophy and thought, we found ourselves bewildered. Our sterile equipment mocked us in our helplessness. We measured without knowing what and why we were measuring. We classified human beings without understanding humanity. We were well on our way to developing a science of trivia, a science of manipulation, a science of pretentious rhetoric and jargon, all the more valued the further it was removed from significant social and psychological realities. We defined valuelessness as an inviolable scientific virtue.

The anguished appeal that power and intelligence be used to protect and enhance the survival of man has been less obvious and demanding in the social and behavioral sciences than in other disciplines, paradoxically, because one would expect that the sciences specifically concerned with the nature and dynamics of man would have led the concern for human survival. The comparative reticence of the social sciences is all the more difficult to understand given their theoretical roots and rationale in the humanities, moral philosophy, and religion.

But then came the revolt of the oppressed, the blacks, the youths, the women, within psychology, and elsewhere. Protesting groups here, like others elsewhere, sought remedies specific to their own interests, yet, behind these confrontations is the assumption that social science is concerned with human values and, therefore, required to seek to direct human behavior toward effectiveness, toward justice, and personal and social stability. These protesters have insisted that disciplined human intelligence—*science*—must be morally responsible to man; that *science*, if it were not to be an accessory to the ultimate obscenity, must enhance the chances of human survival, must provide moral guidelines, in short, must be rehumanized if it were to be adaptive; that psychology must now, after its dalliance, return to its roots, concern itself first with human beings, with values, with ethics, acknowledging that the advances of other sciences—the startling advances in genetics and physics—are contained within moral, ethical parameters to be used for the benefit of mankind.

There are resistances to these demands. There are those who argue—not without some persuasiveness and with the weight of tradition—that the direct involvement of any science with values is contrary to and contaminates scientific objectivity. This violation of objectivity makes science vulnerable to biases, vested interests, and special pleadings which would make science indistinguishable from politics, ideology, and moral philosophy. They insist that the sharing and reallocating of power, the struggle against poverty and deprivation, and racial, class, caste, and sexual injustices are the business of politicians and moralists and revolutionists, and not the business of scientists.

So-called practical men have sought to resolve conflicts of power and status through politics, diplomacy, violence, and systematic military aggression, while religion provided the justification for power. These methods are nonadaptive in this dangerous age. The only method left to be explored is the systematic science of human behavior. Behavioral sciences must seek to understand human social behavior with increasing precision and accuracy and to control the operations of social systems with methods consistent with human values and survival.

A prerequisite for psychology would be operational axioms to guide the exploration of behavior:

1. The behavioral sciences, and psychology, are inherently concerned with values and survival. These concerns cannot be avoided or denied in any systematic effort to understand man and society.

2. Any form of rejection, cruelty, and injustice inflicted upon any group of human beings by any other group of human beings dehumanizes the victims overtly and in more subtle ways dehumanizes the perpetrators.

3. The institutionalization of a system of cruelty and injustice dehumanizes the victims by inhibiting or destroying their positive human potentials; it contributes to the insta-

bility of society by reinforcing negative, destructive, and pathological human characteristics.

4. It is the function of a stable and humane society to remedy and control the destructive potentials of man and to enhance the capacity for creativity as essential to the survival of the human species.

It now appears to be necessary for science to give substance to these ideas and to increase the chances that decision makers will use their power to translate theory into social reality. Toward this end psychology may now be required to pursue even more vigorously the following responsibilities:

1. Define with even greater precision the critical questions on the nature of human aggression, hostility, and cruelty; human love, kindness, and empathy.

2. Determine with precision the effects of various institutional and social arrangements on the reinforcement of positive and negative potentials of man—the meaning of status and hierarchical distinctions and their relationship to injustice and cruelty among men.

3. Understand more clearly the common denominator among such phenomena as primitive tribalism, nationalism, sectarianism, class and caste distinctions, racial and color distinctions, sex and economic distinctions.

4. Seek to understand more confidently the limits of positive modifiability of human beings.

Such a first-stage mobilization of social science has long influenced the work of many behavioral scientists and psychologists. It is now suggested that such tasks be accepted and articulated as central to a cohesive science, and that conceptual cohesion is essential to a morally and socially responsible science. The behavioral scientists would make this knowledge and its practical implications available to policy and decision makers, insisting that the uses of power be consistent with the fundamental values, theories, and the best available knowledge of these sciences.

Morally relevant theories about the nature of man and society must be developed and tested through research, observation, and practice, and then retested and refined through applied social technology, with scientists participating directly in the planning, execution, and evaluation of social programs.

The human values of psychology should be taught at the elementary, secondary, collegiate, graduate, and professional school levels, and the insinuation of the humane values into the teaching of "facts" would seem particularly appropriate in the training of teachers, physicians, lawyers, scientists, and engineers.

Practicing psychologists in schools, hospitals, prisons, government agencies, the military, and other institutions must extend their obligation beyond a narrow definition of professional competence and sensitivity to conditions of cruelty, which dehumanize or destroy human beings. They must speak out against such practices and seek to remedy them without regard to personal risk.

Psychology must now assume its proper role of enhancing and conserving human resources without apology and with full scientific integrity. It must become what it is—the pivotal science of human reality. The social scientist, if he is to meet today's survival challenge, can no longer be permitted to make virtue out of a preoccupation with trivia and an equating of scholarship and scientific research with obfuscation or equivocation. He cannot be permitted to hide his inescapable human values and related truths behind seemingly endless qualifications. Social scientists cannot be permitted to base their claim for superior status on the premise that the prestige of the scientist varies with the distance between the problem which they believe to be worthy of scientific attention and support and the real problems of human beings struggling for justice, equity, and humanity. Nor can they be permitted to hide behind the façade of an elaborate methodology and a preoccupation with methodology for its own sake, a preoccupation with quantification, computers, and a seeming excessive involvement with abstract theorizing. The prestige of social science departments must no longer be allowed to depend on a department's capacity to inculcate in its promising graduate students the belief that a true scientist of human behavior must not take moral positions. The truth of the damage to human beings which results from human cruelties is not qualifiable. The truth that no moral end can be served by the deliberate destruction of human beings becomes a mocking lie by any form of equivocation. In a nuclear age, moral sophistries erode both the fundamental human values essential for a precise social science and make scientific precision unobtainable.

If social scientists do not directly address themselves to the problems of social justice and social responsibility, assuming all of the risks involved, this failure will not be a passive act, but an active act. Social science will have become an accessory to our society's defeat by irrationality, to its victimization by uncontrolled passions and prejudices

[147]

and cruelties. We would be in the position of biologists and medical scientists who contemplated their navels while the world was ravaged by disease.

The development of a science of social responsibility is, I think, the only alternative to the desperation and despair which seems to eat at the innards of so many of our more sensitive students. I believe it is the only answer to the suicidal dance of violence. We, as social scientists, must now say to the world, "Please, let us have a moratorium on irrationality and violence because it is now clear they have solved nothing. Give us a year or two within which to mobilize and reorganize our intellectual disciplines and our sciences, give us a year or two without the cacophony of killings and kidnappings and bombings on campuses or bombings in Southeast Asia within which we can enlist some of our minds in the task of arriving at rational, logical, scientific, and courageous alternatives."

Psychology and psychologists, together with other behavioral scientists, must dare to assume the new and difficult responsibility of serving as ombudsmen for society; they must now be the moral monitors seeking to influence the direction and the quality of the technology of social change, to mobilize its resources to attain social justice and to increase the chances of survival for the species.

If one believes, as I do, that there is nothing absolute or sacred in the prior attempts to restrict science to mere fact-gathering or amoral technology, then one can argue that the role of science can be expanded to include moral guidelines for a desperate society. The most serious threat to the survival of mankind is not now ignorance in the traditional sense, but a morally neutral, that is, an insensitive or inhibited human intelligence.

Unlike the physical or even the biological sciences of the past, the social sciences of the present and the future cannot define objectivity in terms of literal freedom from bias. There must now be the unapologetic bias in favor of the preservation of the human species; a bias in favor of respect for the life and positive potentials of the individual human being; and a bias against any form of destruction, rejection, dehumanization, and cruelty which impairs the capacity of a human being to live and love and contribute to the welfare of other human beings.

EPILOGUE:

PATHOS OF POWER,
A PSYCHOLOGICAL
PERSPECTIVE

A SEARCH FOR congruence and consistency among the various aspects of one's being would seem mandatory, if not inevitable, for those who are arrogant enough to use the discipline of psychology to legitimize their functioning. The luxury and safety of defining scientific objectivity in terms of a detached, disciplined, isolated, and amoral use of human intelligence is not available to those who have chosen to work in the social, psychological, and behavioral sciences, or for that matter in the biological and medical sciences.

Psychological phenomena do not seem to consist of absolute realities. Their reality is the tantalizing, persistent reality of the subjective. This fact of relativistic reality differentiates the science of psychology from all other sciences. This difference between psychology and the physical sciences remains in spite of the fact that the evidence of all sciences—indeed, the inevitable basis of all knowledge—must be filtered through the limits of human observational powers and refined by limited human intelligence.

Psychologists and other social scientists must seek to organize their findings within a conceptual framework which will, perhaps, expand knowledge and broaden and deepen insights into the nature of man and his society. There remains, also, for psychology, the ultimate test of the validity of all sciences—a demonstration of an effective technology, the ability to predict or control the phenomena which we purport to understand. The critical questions for a contemporary science of psychology and for other behavioral sciences are these: What are their contributions to the understanding and control of the behavior of human beings? How can the knowledge, the insights, and the related technology contribute directly or indirectly to effectiveness of individual human beings and to stability in human society, and increase the chances of survival of the human species?

These are important questions and there is now a special urgency in finding and implementing affirmative answers to them within the context of respect for human values. Those who try cannot divorce their analyses and insights from the total complexity of their own being. What follows is my own attempt to share with others the process—the intellectual and emotional turbulence—by which my own views and suggestions concerning the dynamics of man and society emerged.

INFLUENCE OF EARLY RESEARCH ON DEVELOPING IDEAS

My first serious scientific involvement in the larger theoretical concerns with the nature of man and society resulted from the need to interpret the findings of early research on the nature and development of the self and the problems of

[154]

ego and racial identification in which I was a collaborator with my wife, Dr. Mamie Clark. This fascinating and somewhat illusive "pure" research problem was initially my wife's master's thesis problem. As she saw the larger implications of the first stages of this work, she was kind enough to invite me to join her in a more probing empirical and theoretical exploration of the nature and determinants of the self-image.

As we collected and analyzed the data we obtained, we became impressed with the implications of the observation that in the initial stages of the emerging sense of self in children the substance and the dynamics of the functioning ego were determined almost exclusively by external pressures, determinants, and evaluative agents. These findings proved to be the first clues to insights about the fragility, vulnerability, dependence, indeed, the pathos of the human ego. This early research on the emergence of self-awareness and preference in Negro children illuminated for us the larger pattern of problems related to ego development in human beings. Among these insights were:

- The functional substance of the self is not indigenous to the human organism, but is determined by the nature and pattern of human interaction as this is influenced by the status of the individual in a familial and social hierarchical system, by the way the individual is perceived and treated.
- The qualitative effect of the external determinants of the individual's sense of self is inevitably evaluative; i.e., the resulting emerging self-image brings with it a positive or negative sense of the worth of self.
- This positive or negative evaluative component of self is pivotal—and in its most primary and basic sense is not

controlled by the individual himself but by others over whom he has no control.

- In the most formative and susceptible stage of a child's life, that period within which there is the beginning of the ability to cope with ideas, the idea of the self and the worth and status of the self are inextricable.
- This initial external definition of the nature, worth, and status of self tends to persist throughout the life of the individual; it is reinforced by consistent experiences, internalized as the core of personality, and it establishes the patterns of defense and protection which the individual uses in interpersonal and other forms of social interaction.
- In spite of the above, human beings—except those who have been totally defeated by negative evaluation of others and by consistent rejection or those who are organically deficient—persist in the struggle for self-affirmation and the attainment of that minimum self-esteem required to continue to function as a human being. And it remains one of the mysteries of psychological science that individual human beings differ— whether markedly or minimally is still open to question —in the physical equipment, intellectual strengths, and general life force, and in other personal resources, which they can mobilize in the continuing struggle for personal affirmation and an effective self-esteem.

My research on the social and attitudinal factors influencing memory and recall—related to the larger problem of the effect of social factors on perception and cognition—tended to reinforce my ideas on the fragility of the human ego. This early study, conducted in partial fulfillment for the Ph.D. at

Columbia University, incidentally, anticipated some of the later research on cognitive styles and foreshadowed some of the concerns of the women's liberation movement in the finding that men and women differed markedly in the recall of the activities of a dominant woman. The finding that human beings tended to recall events in terms consistent with their attitudes and within the context of their personalities seemed to provide further supportive evidence of the human need to use all available sensory and intellective resources in the attempt to obscure the tenuousness of our being—and to assert an inner certainty and absoluteness as having reality and existence primarily because they are asserted.

Further studies of the effects of social pressures and the consequences of rejection and acceptance of individuals and groups by the larger society culminated in the publication of *Dark Ghetto*. While the writing of *Dark Ghetto* drew on earlier research insights, this specific study of the psychological effects of a ghetto community resulted in a more focused picture of the effects of adverse, persistent negatives on the distortion of personality and on the impairment of psychological effectiveness of the victims of persistent rejection. Here again, the persistent fact of the fragility and vulnerability of the human ego, somewhat tempered by insights concerning the counterstruggle for self-esteem and the resilience of human beings, was reinforced.

The earlier studies of the development of self-identification and evaluation in children with Mamie Clark were not motivated by or conducted with any direct concern for their applied or policy implications and consequences. The fact that the United States Supreme Court in handing down the *Brown* decision in May 1954 cited these findings and other relevant research which I summarized in the document *The Effects of Prejudice a..d Discrimination on Personality Development*[1] was a gratifying illustration of the possibility that even in the social and psychological sciences what is called "pure" research can sometimes have some direct social policy and applied social change effects. The *Dark Ghetto* community psychology research, on the other hand, from its inception was clearly motivated by the desire to influence social policy and the decisions of those with power to facilitate, block, or determine the rate of desired social change. The *Dark Ghetto* study cannot be described with candor as an exercise in "pure" research on the problem of culture and personality. This study of the dynamics of a systematically dehumanizing community on the humanity and effectiveness of the personalities confined within it was not conducted without concern for the implications of these findings for social justice and social change. The Harlem Youth Opportunities (HARYOU) report, *Youth in the Ghetto,* expanded and revised into *Dark Ghetto,* had been modeled after investigations in public health and preventive medicine. These reports did seek to analyze and describe the effects of social policy and practice; to diagnose the nature and manifestations of social instability; and to suggest remedies for the persistent social insensitivities and resulting pathologies which robbed human beings of self-esteem, which reinforced negative self-images and destroyed the potential for personal and social effectiveness.

In a recent analysis of a sample of antipoverty programs—

1. *The Effects of Prejudice and Discrimination on Personality Development.* Fact-finding Report, Mid-Century White House Conference on Children and Youth, Washington, D.C., Federal Security Agency, Children's Bureau, 1950.

A *Relevant War Against Poverty*, coauthored with Jeannette Hopkins—it was clear that the *Dark Ghetto* findings had influenced the rationale and programmatic structure of federally funded antipoverty and community-based action programs. But this detailed study of these programs within the first two years of the programs' existence predicted their failure by revealing the controlling and inhibiting fact that those human beings with power are deeply unwilling or unable to share even a modicum of real power with those who have been powerless. The poor and the powerless are perceived and treated as if they are objects to be manipulated, taunted, played with, and punished by those with power. They are required to be grateful for the verbalizations and the crumbs of power—and are rejected as incorrigibly inferior, childlike, or barbaric if they rebel against and otherwise disturb the convenience of their more powerful benefactors. Antipoverty programs based upon these social realities were doomed to failure because they reflected a total lack of commitment to eliminate poverty, to share power with the powerless. Above all, they reflected the inability of the decision makers and the society as a whole to change the set of perceiving inferior human beings. These programs did not want to, and would not, operate in terms of the rationale and the goals of the potential equality of all human beings. They did not seek to accept and strengthen the humanity of the deprived through compassion, empathy, and a serious sharing of power.

An Emerging Conceptual Framework

There is no doubt that these research projects, the developing ideas, and the related forms of social action were influenced most fundamentally by the psychodynamic theories of Alfred Adler. It was the late Francis Cecil Sumner, professor of psychology at Howard University, who first introduced me as an undergraduate to the promises of the science of psychology for the understanding of man and society. It was he who gave me my first serious appreciation of the complexities of the meanings of humanity. In his characteristic style Professor Sumner presented Adler's thoughts within the framework of other psychoanalytic and psychodynamic theories and within the larger context of religion and philosophy. This experience had a profound influence upon my thoughts, my research, and my professional and personal action.

Gestalt, holistic, and organismic theories also exerted a strong influence on my developing ideas. Kurt Goldstein's ability to interpret his observations of the meaning of the symptoms of the brain-injured patients in a unified psychodynamic perspective of the struggle of human beings to maintain an integrated ego—to minimize their deficiencies and maximize their available assets—reinforced the basic significance of Adlerian and organismic theory in my thinking. As one of Goldstein's graduate students at Columbia University, I struggled to understand his lectures. I admired his ability to present and document a holistic, organismic view of man as a biosocial organism.

In spite of the more dramatic, fashionable, provocative, and, in many respects, profound ideas of Freud, my thoughts and scientific activities were only peripherally influenced by the fundamental Freudian premises. My persistent concerns with the effects of the social system on the functioning and effectiveness of individuals and groups propelled me more toward the social psychological emphasis of Adler and made me somewhat resistant to the Freudian emphasis on deeper intrapsychic dynamics. In its emphasis on innate instinctive processes and its related inability to emphasize the effects of social problems and continued social pressures on the individual's effectiveness, traditional Freudian theory seemed inadequate—limited and constricted—for a dynamic social psychology. Freudian theory does not appear to offer a theoretical basis for a psychology concerned with social change or a psychotechnology other than one-to-one psychoanalytic therapy. Adler's concern with man's social interaction and his emphasis on the human struggle for self-esteem were much more compatible with my main research and action in seeking a humane technology to enhance the chances of humanity among men. The quest for a more enlightened social policy, morally and rationally determined social change, could not proceed from the premise that man is a totally or primarily nonrational organism whose most powerful drives are instinctive and animalistic. My resistance to the Freudian perspective of man and society was not unlike the objections of the late Gordon Allport, who refused to accept the Freudian view of man as an essentially nonrational being. Allport insisted that the rational components of the complexities of human motivation must be given at least an equal if not a dominant role with the nonrational.

The core Adlerian idea which persists in its influence on my thinking concerns the nature of psychological power in understanding human beings and human society. Bertrand Russell's assertion that "the fundamental concept in social science is Power, in the same sense in which Energy is a fundamental concept in physics" reinforced the influence of Adlerian theory in my thinking.

In an earlier exploration I defined the phenomenon of

social power operationally as "the force or energy required to bring about, to sustain or to prevent social, political or economic change." As my research and my interest in social change tended to converge and eventually fuse, I became preoccupied with the problem of a theory of social power as a unifying conceptual framework. More and more I tended to see social power, in its manifest forms, as that force or combination of forces which facilitated, blocked, or determined the rate and direction of social change. In a dynamic social situation power expresses itself as a Gestalt or a quantum expression of the power aspirations and competition among significant individuals and groups.

Observations of the manifestations of power in social and institutional situations suggested that one could not hope to understand the dynamics of social power without trying to understand competition for power and the complex pattern of conflicts between power and competition on the one hand and love, kindness, and rationality on the other hand. These interrelated problems, conflicts, and contradictions reveal the stark pathos of power and betray the predicament of the human ego.

The pathetic vulnerability of the human ego may be illustrated by the insight that the most ruthless, power-competitive individual may be driven by an insatiable need to be loved and accepted by others. Nowhere can such an individual obtain enough actual power to disguise from himself the essential fact—the intolerable fact—of his own essential inner powerlessness. In such extreme cases the drive for power blocks or destroys the capacity to love and be loved and thereby strengthens the cycle of self-defeating obsession with power.

A contemporary example of human power pathos is the

anguished cries of the advocates of Black Power. It is clear that the verbalizations of such power betray the reality of powerlessness. The frustrations, the rejection, the denial of the ability to fulfill legitimate aspirations are compensated for among extreme advocates of Black Power by the posture and the delusional rhetoric of a power persistently denied. This insight into the nature of this particular form of diversionary pseudo power paradoxically led me into a more empathic understanding of the human pathos and psychological predicament of white racial extremists. Through my understanding and racial identification with compensatory black extremists, I came to understand that whites who need to use the crutches of racial cruelty and extremism are also forlorn, deprived, desperately pathetic human beings.

When one dares to confront the many examples of the mocking pathos of power, one finds oneself going beyond Adler even while remaining dependent upon fundamental Adlerian insights. The Adlerian emphasis on the affirmative struggle for self-esteem and status becomes intensified by the disturbing, almost intolerable reality that a positive self-esteem, what Freud calls narcissism, is not determined by forces inherent within the human organism, but is dependent upon external supports and reinforcements, and controlled by the judgments of others who themselves are afflicted with the universal human anxiety of self-doubt.

The essence of the human predicament is the inescapable reality that the human ego is a most fragile and delicate phenomenon. It is difficult, if not impossible, to be human without embarrassment—an embarrassment rooted in the ever-imminent and intolerable insight into the reality of the tenuousness and transitory quality of the all-powerful and at the same time powerless human ego.

Consciousness provides the flimsy base of the human ego. All we seem to know about the human cortical cells whose mysterious interactions form the base of consciousness is that they are unique among all of the combinations of matter and energy known to exist in the universe. They make possible perception, awareness, evaluation, self-reflection, anxiety, reflection on the past, and anticipation of the future. They make the human ego real—sometimes painfully real. They create and validate humanity and they sustain the struggle for justice and decency in human relationships even as they provide the basis for rationalizing cruelties and inhumanity.

To make these abstractions real, these mysterious human cortical cells require a rather specific biochemical environment. They require that oxygen and nourishment be provided and regulated through an elaborate capillary system. The unstable equilibrium within and around these cells must be maintained within a tolerable range of variation if the human ego and the complexities of function and continuity inherent in the sense of self are to be sustained.

The normal functioning and the identity of the self can be disrupted through one or any combination of disturbances within the internal environment. Disruption in continuity of a personal identity—loss of social and psychological continuity and existence—can occur in spite of the continuation of biological existence if there is any significant deprivation in the specific biochemical requirements of these cortical cells. With such deprivation there can be change in temperament and fundamental changes in the threshold of positive and negative responses or sensitivity to external environmental forces.

These cortical cells hold within them the keys to the

mystery of the definition and the functional quality of the self. They control, by their ability to intensify, reduce, or obliterate, the basic reality that is the self. And they are fragile. And it is upon the basis of their fragility that the human ego remains a delicate thing. To be human is not determined merely by the concretes of sensory functions, neural integration, and skeletal muscular behavior of the human organism. The essence of being human is defined by the normal functioning of the uniquely complex human being.

These insights are fraught with anxieties and probably should best be handled by denial or repression. Even before the ennui of youth became a fashionable topic of discussion, one of my students suggested in a brilliant paper for my class in Human Motivation that the fundamental fear of man was the fear of confronting the *void within*. The sense of inner emptiness, a sense of limited experiential time, a sense of essential powerlessness, as the basic realities of the human experience—these are not tolerable insights. They must be compensated for with more positive, substantive concepts of self. Fortunately, the human brain which made this human predicament possible can also create, invent, or rationalize ideational substance up to and including indefinite continuity for the human ego.

The idea of the void within is abhorrent. The void must be filled. The creative activities of man—his religion, his philosophy, his art, his literature, his buildings, his cults, his cruelties, his science, his technologies—are attempts to fill this void or to obscure its existence. Human civilizations are objectifications of the inner turbulence of man. In proving to himself that his life is more than the continuous transformation of one form of biological and chemical energy into other

[165]

forms of physical and behavioral energy, man seems compelled to mobilize and use psychological and social power constructively or destructively. The alternative would be to accept a level of desperation and stagnation indistinguishable from psychological death.

Among the paradoxes of the human predicament is that these disturbing insights, complicated as they are by the inevitability of evaluation inherent in the operation of human consciousness, demand that human beings define human existence in terms greater than an interval between the accidents of conception and birth and the infinite nothingness of death. The mysterious power and forces which culminate in human consciousness insist that to be human is to be more than the awesome and finite mystery of existential life. Human beings must affirm humanity and assert that there is purpose to and sacredness to human life despite all threatening evidence to the contrary. This is the dynamic and the compensatory pathos of power. Affirmation-in-spite-of is the common denominator of human creativity and destructiveness; of human love and kindness and human hostility and cruelty; of human compassion and human egocentric posturing and bombast. Affirmation-in-spite-of provides the basis for all that is sacred and barbaric in man.

In his discussion of the Psychic Fictions which are essential in providing substance to human psychological existence, Adler stated in his *Understanding Human Nature:*

> We can realize how relative are the values of sensations, when not even these are absolute quantities; these elements of our psychic activity are influenced by the striving for a definite goal, our very perceptions are prejudiced by it, and are chosen, so to speak, with a secret

hint at the final goal toward which the personality is striving.

We orient ourselves according to a fixed point which we have artificially created, which does not in reality exist, a fiction. This assumption is necessary because of the inadequacy of our psychic life. . . . In the case of all psychic fictions we have to do with the following: we assume a fixed point even though closer observation forces us to admit that it does not exist. The purpose of this assumption is simply to orient ourselves in the chaos of existence, so that we can arrive at some apperception of relative values. The advantage is that we can categorize every sensation and every sentiment according to this fixed point, once we have assumed it.

These Psychic Fictions, these ideational inventions and objective creations of man which constitute his culture and civilizations, ordinarily seem sufficient to quell temporarily the incipient anguish of the imminence of nonbeing. They frequently postpone the ultimate embarrassment of the acceptance of personal and collective nonimportance.

Of all the compensatory protective agents invented or created by the human brain as a cushion against the intolerable realities of human flimsiness, probably the most flexible and effective has been the idea of God. Man has invested God with both omnipotence and permanence. An analysis of the characteristics of God, the powers and functions of God, betrays the pathos and the vulnerability of man. One of the most important functions of God is protection of man against accepting and coming to terms with the realities of human limitations. In a most literal and basic psychological sense, God is the primary source of power for man. Man created God to create man with introjective strengths, with solidity, and with purpose and substance. To perform this awesome and important task there must be an ideationally literal God. If for no other reason, therefore, God is not only not dead, man cannot permit God to die. If God were to die, human beings would have to die psychologically, even though they were alive as organisms.

The importance of God as a shield against the fragility of the ego is revealed in the demigods, the directly observable gods created by the human mind and invested with protective power. Magicians, medicine men, priests, bishops, kings, generals, father figures, movie stars, all serve similar divine functions. These charismatic figures, these personifications of power, are anointed with virtues and powers beyond those found in ordinary men. Through identification with these demigods and their projected power, the average man can obscure his own weaknesses and affirm his ego. Some of these human gods internalize the godlike attributes. They come to believe and behave as if they are gods—or engage in a continuous struggle against this tantalizing temptation. From this point of view, paradox emerges as the major characteristic or quality of a bemused God—a God of the inescapable practical joke of the human predicament.

Human beings have invented and emotionally identified with various groups in order to play a similar protective and power-broker function. Tribes, cults, religions, nations, and their coercive and protective dogmas and ideologies may be seen as group gods, bestowing substance and strengths upon individuals otherwise vulnerable. The strength and power of a group seem directly proportional to its success in compensating for the fragility of its individual members or in obscuring their insignificance and pathos. These benefits appear to grow if the group demonstrates an ability to exercise power over other groups of human beings and inflict cruelty upon them.

SOCIAL POWER: A STRUGGLE FOR INTEGRATION
FOR ORGANISMIC AND SOCIAL SYSTEMS

There is the tendency among many of us who are concerned with studying more systematically the crucial role of social power in human affairs to present our case as if power is the only significant motivational force and as if it can operate in isolation from the total complexity of structure and integrated functions of organismic and social systems.

A realistic view of social power requires that it be seen as a pervasive and integrative force, operating in relationship to other forces in the dynamic constellation of the human personality.

Personality is defined here as the characteristic way in which the individual human organism mobilizes and uses its available resources in its struggle for survival, satisfaction, status, meaning, and moral integrity. This definition suggests a hierarchy of motivation in which power or status needs lie between the more primitive drives toward survival and sensual satisfactions and the uniquely human motives of the quest for meaning and moral integrity. Power may, therefore, operate toward either end of the continuum to reinforce or make dominant either the primitive or the human. Power may make stark and rigid, or determine fixation or regression; and it may determine the pattern of relationship among the motivational levels. It can intensify, obscure, or contaminate one or more motives in the dynamic system of personality. Power and status needs can determine whether other needs will be gratified in animalistic, egocentric, or nonadaptive ways or in human, empathic, and socially constructive channels.

This is the dilemma of power whence the pathos of power arises.

THE CONTEMPORARY CRISIS OF THE PATHOS OF POWER

Power cannot be exercised without inducing reaction or counter-reaction. Social power almost always involves confrontations and conflicts; and these lead usually to accommodation, with or without residual resentment; or to acute defiance, sporadic counter-reaction, or prolonged and smoldering resistance. And this, in turn, leads back to conflict—this is the psychodynamic base for the cycle of power.

The rewards of power are transitory; and the gratifications of power and status needs are frequently nonadaptive and self-defeating. Power exhibits the symptoms of nonadaptive pathos and futility:

1. When the exercise of power does not increase, or when it interferes with, the chances of gratifying the more basic needs of survival and satisfaction.
2. When the exercise of power is ambiguous, random, arbitrary, regressive, disproportionately intense, and rigid in spite of consequences.
3. When the exercise of power becomes so functionally autonomous and extreme in intensity that it subverts and perverts the critical, rational, and moral capacities of individuals and groups.
4. When the attainment of the symbols of power or the unchallenged actuality of power results in a sense of

futility and ennui and the dissipation of the desire or the capacity to use power constructively or creatively.

The continuation, intensification, and cumulative effect of any combination of these symptoms is a major threat to the organism or the social system. This crisis betrays the fact that the power system has become self-directing and is no longer controlled by the organism and social system to serve their adaptive needs. The survival of the system would then seem to depend upon its capacity to redirect these power drives and channel their energy toward constructive ends within the imperative period of time.

Certainly, the normal brain has the necessary survival alert systems that ordinarily can be engaged to prevent the organism from pursuing rigidly the paths of self-destruction. Whether the human brain can resolve the contemporary survival crises of social power positively and constructively is in doubt. It is a mocking fact that the human brain can rationalize intellectually and morally in support of a non-adaptive, ultimately destructive use of social power. It can invent ideational, delusional realities that provide the crutches for the fragile human ego. It can justify human pomp and pretense while nonrational forces propel man toward disaster. But the human brain is also the only source of positive alternatives—alternatives to personal anxieties, humiliations, intergroup tensions, violence; alternatives to suicide, homicide, and the barbarities of war.

Contemporary man's technological mastery of matter and energy, with the related ultimate thermonuclear weaponry, confronts us with this fact: it is now possible to destroy the human species through the nonadaptive use of human intelligence and the destructive, pathetic use of social power.

This threat is so ultimate and so urgent that human beings seek to deny or repress it. But it does exist. And it must be coped with if human beings are to function without the gnawing and debilitating anxieties inherent in the imminence of extinction.

This survival crisis requires immediate mobilization of all that is positive within man to provide us with the time to prevent man from destroying the human species—the time to evolve and to develop a more stable organismic base for the rational and moral exercise of social power.

THE ERA OF PSYCHOTECHNOLOGY

The present generation of human beings is required to develop psychological and social sciences with that degree of precision, predictability, and moral control essential to survival. The awesome advances in the physical and biological sciences have made psychotechnology imperative. Man can no longer afford the luxuries of a leisurely, trial-and-error, trivia-dominated approach to the behavioral sciences. The behavioral sciences are now the critical sciences; they will determine the answer to the ultimate moral question of human survival.

The psychological and social sciences must enable us to control the animalistic, barbaric, and primitive propensities in man and subordinate these negatives to the uniquely human moral and ethical characteristics of love, kindness, and empathy. The redirecting of power away from the absurd and the pathetic and the self-defeating can be and now must be seen as a responsibility and goal of science and psychotechnology. We can no longer afford to rely solely upon the traditional pre-scientific attempts to contain human cruelty and destructiveness. The techniques and appeals of religion, moral philosophy, law, and education seemed appropriate and civilized approaches to the control of man's primitive and egocentric behavior in a pre-nuclear age. They are, in themselves, no longer appropriate because they permit too wide a margin of error and a degree of unpredictability that is rationally inconsistent with the present survival urgency. Furthermore, moral verbalizations of the past have been prostituted by the pathos of power; they have been perverted by the pretenses of rationality in the service of inhumanity, even barbarity.

The traditional perspective and training of psychologists, educators, and moral philosophers would lead them to continue to argue that moral controls of human primitive and egocentric impulses depend on redoubling our efforts to develop more effective forms of moral education designed to produce individual human beings of ethical autonomy and integrity. They would argue that it is still possible to preserve human civilization by training human beings toward a higher quality of interpersonal relationships; by developing within individual human beings greater personal and social effectiveness through greater ego strengths. They would continue to assert that a variety of behavioral modification techniques, imposed particularly in childhood, could be expected to reinforce altruism, empathy, and group commitment and to subordinate egocentricity in normal human beings.

An objective appraisal of the results of these approaches to a control of the negatives in man and the enhancement of his positives would seem to suggest that not only are the results of such approaches unpredictable, but that continuous reinforcement and a prolonged period of time are required in order to demonstrate positive results. We do not now appear to have such time.

The era of psychotechnology coincides with the abrupt recognition of the limits of the time within which the human brain can discover and use that knowledge which is requisite to control, protect, and affirm humanity with precision and predictability. Already neurophysiological, biochemical, and psychopharmacological and psychological research has put forward provocative and suggestive findings. The work on the effects of direct stimulation of certain areas of the brain; the role of specific areas of the mid-brain in controlling certain affects; the impact of certain drugs on exciting, tranquilizing, or depressing the emotional and motivational levels of the individual; and the effects of externally induced behavioral changes on internal biochemistry of the organism—these and other findings suggest that we might be on the threshold of a scientific biochemical intervention which could stabilize and make dominant the moral and ethical propensities of man and subordinate, if not eliminate, his negative and primitive behavioral tendencies.

Upon the basis of the presently available evidence, it is reasonable to believe that this type of precise, direct psychotechnological intervention designed to strengthen man's moral and positive human characteristics could be ready to be implemented within a few years and with a fraction of the cost required to produce the atom bomb, a minute part of the cost of our recent explorations in outer space.

I am suggesting that, with the mobilization of scientific personnel, financial resources, and research facilities, it is now possible—as it is imperative—to reduce human anxieties, tensions, hostilities, violence, cruelty, and the destructive power irrationalities which are the basis of wars. This contemporary approach to assuring the survival of the human species offers a scientific basis for William James's philosophical wish for a moral equivalent or alternative to wars.

In reducing the negative and enhancing the positive potentials in human beings, serious political organizational and administrative problems would need to be resolved, and numerous important psychological barriers would need to be faced and overcome with realism and respect for that essential humanity which differentiates human beings from mere organisms or living machines. The process and techniques of direct biochemical intervention, or any form of effective psychotechnology, must take into account the totality, the interrelatedness, the complex Gestalt of the human motivational, affective, and cognitive system. In seeking to enhance empathy and kindness and to reduce the cruel and the barbaric in man, psychotechnology must refrain from destroying the creative, evaluative, and selective capacities of human beings. Without the desire to explore, to reorganize things and ideas, to vary moods, and to produce at least with the illusion of flexibility and volition, the human being would indeed be an empty organic vessel and it would be difficult to justify mere survival under such conditions. This suggested psychotechnological intervention must be not only precise and predictable but affirmatively humane. This new era of the psychological sciences must bring to science an essential new dimension—an inviolable sense of moral responsibility.

The implications of this psychotechnological intervention are of such immense significance as to demand that the most careful and rigorous planning, research, and testing precede any attempts to apply these findings on a larger scale. Because the program would be concerned with uniquely human problems the pre-test subjects would have to be human beings. The implications of an effective psychotechnology for the control of criminal behavior and the amelioration of the moral insensitivities which produce reactive criminality are clear. There would seem, therefore, to be moral and rational justification for the use of compulsive criminals as pre-test subjects in research on intervention in and control of human moral behavior. This suggestion is based upon the assumption that no human being who is not impelled by internal, biochemical, or external, social forces—or some combination of both—would choose to be a criminal if he were provided with options.

It is a fact that a few men in the leadership positions in the industrialized nations of the world now have the power to determine among themselves, through collaboration or competition, the survival or extinction of human civilization. They can, in fact, exercise this power only within the present limitations of the pathos and contradictions of power which can be directed to temporary good or unpredictable ultimate evil. We cannot predict the personal and emotional stability of these leaders who have life and death power over mankind. Nor do we now understand if there is a relationship between those personal characteristics required for success in gaining political and governmental power and those characteristics required for personal, emotional, and moral stability. The masses of human beings must now live and work in faith and hope, with denial of the danger, and with acceptance of the odds that their powerful leaders will have the strength to use their power wisely and morally.

It would seem logical then that a requirement should be

imposed upon all power-controlling leaders and those who aspire to such leadership that they accept and use the earliest perfected form of psychotechnological, biochemical intervention which would assure their use of power affirmatively, and reduce or block the possibility of their using power destructively. Such psychotechnological medication would be an internally imposed disarmament. It would assure that there would be no absurd or barbaric use of power. It would provide the masses of human beings with the security that their leaders would not or could not sacrifice them on the altars of their personal ego pathos, their vulnerability and instability.

It is possible to object to the era of psychotechnology on "moral" grounds and to assert that these suggestions are repugnant because they are manipulative and will take away from man his natural right to make errors—even those errors which perpetrate cruelties and destruction upon other human beings. In the light of the realities of and possible consequences of nuclear weaponry, these allegedly moral arguments seem mockingly, pathetically immoral. Man could afford to indulge in such abstract, pre-scientific moralizing in the past when his most destructive weapons were clubs, bows and arrows, or even gunpowder. To perpetuate such thinking in an age when nuclear weapons are capable of destroying millions of human beings in a single, irrational man-made event would seem to reflect self-defeating and immoral rigidity.

There could be the further objection that biochemical intervention into the inner psychological recesses of motivation, temperament, and behavior is an unacceptable, intolerable tampering with the natural or God-given characteristics

[177]

of man. To support this objection the negative connotations presently associated with discussions of drugs and the drug culture, particularly among young people, could be invoked. One could also object on the ground that under the guise of an imperative psychotechnology the strategy suggested here would simply drug the masses and their leaders, thus producing another form of utopian mechanization of human beings.

These objections seem to be based upon a misconception of the purposes and methods of medical science. Physical diseases are controlled through medication prescribed by doctors to help the body overcome the detrimental effects of bacteria or viruses—or to help the organism restore that balance of internal biochemical environment necessary for health and effectiveness. Medicines are used to treat the victims of diseases, but they are also employed preventively in the form of vaccines. All drugs used therapeutically—all medicines are drugs—are forms of intervention to influence and control the natural processes of disease. Appropriate selective medication to assure psychological health and moral integrity is now imperative for the survival of human society.

The Era of Psychotechnology, imposed upon man by the advances of the physical sciences, cannot now be avoided. It must be used affirmatively, wisely, and with compassion. To fulfill these requirements it must have a sound scientific, factual base. It must also be firmly rooted in rational morality. It must respect and enhance that which is uniquely human in man—those positive qualities that promise a future of human grandeur. In meeting these and related requirements, a rigorous, tough-minded science and technology of psychology will save man from the more destructive consequences of his absurdities and propensities—the pathos of power—and will provide him with the time necessary to evolve and stabilize those centers of his brain which will make social morality and human survival no longer a matter of chance.

INDEX

About the Author

Kenneth B. Clark has sought to carry out his own philosophy of a science of social responsibility. He is a scholar who is committed to research and diagnosis of his society, to teaching and writing, and to action. He holds posts that reflect these concerns—Distinguished Professor of Psychology of the City University of New York, president of MARC (Metropolitan Applied Research Center, Inc.); he is active in numerous organizations, a member of the Board of Regents of New York State, a trustee of the University of Chicago, a member of the boards of Rand (New York), the New York State Urban Development Corporation, and Harper & Row. He is past president of the American Psychological Association and of the Society for the Psychological Study of Social Issues, served as consultant to the NAACP, the State Department, and a number of foundations, corporations, and educational institutions. He is author of *Dark Ghetto: Dilemmas of Social Power*, *A Relevant War Against Poverty* with Jeannette Hopkins, and *Prejudice and Your Child*, and coeditor with Talcott Parsons of *The Negro American*.